Good
News!

CORWIN
PRESS

The Corwin Press logo—a raven striding across an open book—represents the happy union of courage and learning. We are a professional-level publisher of books and journals for K–12 educators, and we are committed to creating and providing resources that embody these qualities. Corwin's motto is "Success for All Learners."

Good News!

How to Get the Best Possible Media Coverage for Your School

Gail A. Conners

CORWIN PRESS, INC.
A Sage Publications Company
Thousand Oaks, California

For information:

Corwin Press, Inc.
A Sage Publications Company
2455 Teller Road
Thousand Oaks, California 91320
E-mail: order@corwinpress.com

Sage Publications Ltd.
6 Bonhill Street
London EC2A 4PU
United Kingdom

Sage Publications India Pvt. Ltd.
M-32 Market
Greater Kailash I
New Delhi 110 048 India

Printed in the United States of America

Library of Congress Cataloging-in-Publication Data

Conners, Gail A.
    Good news! : How to get the best possible media coverage for your school /
by Gail A. Conners
        p.   cm.
    Includes bibliographical references.
    ISBN 0-7619-7506-3 (cloth: alk. paper)
    ISBN 0-7619-7507-1 (pbk.: alk. paper)
    1. Schools—Public relations—United States.   2. Community and
school—United States.   3. Education in mass media.   I. Title.
    LB2847 .C65   2000
    659.2'9371—dc21   99-050518

This book is printed on acid-free paper.

00   01   02   03   04   05   06   7   6   5   4   3   2   1

Corwin Editorial Assistant: Catherine Kantor
Production Editor: Denise Santoyo
Editorial Assistant: Victoria Cheng
Typesetter/Designer: Lynn Miyata/Tina Hill
Cover Designer: Oscar Desierto

Contents

Exhibits

Preface

The business of education is often fraught with complexities. Conveying that information to the potentially affected interest groups (e.g., taxpayers, parents, employees) of a school or district can be a challenge, but it's a necessary step in developing a sound communications program that will go a long way toward building credibility with the public and the media. Public support is contingent on understanding what a school or district is attempting to accomplish.

I mention credibility because it is the heart of *Good News! How to Get the Best Possible Media Coverage for Your School*. Schools are public entities and, as such, often subject to criticism. People inherently distrust any government agency—including educational ones. Without credibility and demonstrative accountability, a school or district will fail in getting projects off the ground or support for difficult decisions. The "feel good news," such as science fairs, reading programs, and special speakers, will not find a media outlet if schools shun the media when asked about "hard news" items such as teacher strikes, teen violence, or tax increases.

Good News! is a "rule of thumb" for individuals in educational communications who want to maximize their resources. Whether you are an educator charged with media relations or a practitioner who might want to read more about other schools handling similar situations, you will find helpful information.

Schools have two options regarding the media: (a) open a two-way process for clear, honest communication; or (b) have an adversarial relationship based on distrust and misinformation. The latter is a no-win situation. I know. I spent 7 years as a public information specialist to the City School District of Albany, New York. If a district responds to hard news or difficult issues in a constructive, honest way, that will do more to build a bank of credibility with its public than any "feel good" press release could.

While in Albany, I received training from Hans and Annemarie Bleiker, a couple who travel across the country offering citizen participation workshops for public officials and other professionals accountable to the public. Their Systematic Development of Informed Consent (SDIC) workshop entirely changed my approach to media and community relations. After years of research, the Bleikers developed fundamental principles and methods for building informed consent among a public agency's interest groups (including opponents) with proven success. The cornerstone of SDIC is *The Bleiker Lifepreserver*, a set of guidelines to use in handling difficult situations with the public and the media. SDIC, The Bleiker Lifepreserver, and their applications to communications are the foundations of this book. Once you grasp their focus, it is much easier to develop a communications plan, create a positive relationship with the media, and handle a crisis when it does occur. After many years as a communications professional, I now assess a public relations challenge with "How can I Bleiker this?"

Good News! offers practical, "real world" approaches to many of the dilemmas facing educators and practitioners today. It is not steeped in research, but rather in case studies from those in education and the media. Schools and districts vary in size and public expectation, but *Good News!* is about basic public relations truths from the very people who deal with them on a daily basis.

Chapter 1 delves into the role of The Bleiker Lifepreserver, how to use it, and how the training has helped several public institutions. The Bleiker Lifepreserver is an integral element throughout the book and essential to any public agency's communications efforts.

Going a step farther, Chapter 2 focuses more on developing credibility and accountability and their importance in a school's overall communications approach.

Chapter 3 illustrates how to combine The Bleiker Lifepreserver and accountability into a communications plan that will help a school or district map out a strategic plan in getting out the good news and handling the hard news.

Chapter 4 outlines a comprehensive approach in how to build a relationship with the media; how to convey information in a clear, concise way; how to obtain positive media coverage through concrete examples; how to work with the media when the thorniest of issues arise; and how the media operate.

Chapter 5 outlines crisis communications and what educators can do to prepare themselves and their community when a catastrophe occurs. As more incidents of school violence immobilize the country, schools need to prepare for a worst-case scenario by drafting and implementing crisis communications plans. So, when trauma does befall a school, administrators will act swiftly and accordingly and, one hopes, lessen the impact of the crisis.

Although *Good News!* is primarily about media relations, schools can take advantage of many other communications tools at their disposal to help spread the word. Chapter 6 illustrates how school-business partnerships can lead to greater press opportunities, and Chapter 7 offers tips on creating more effective newsletters and Web sites.

Schools cannot rely solely on the media to deliver accurate information. In fact, the media alone will not change public perception. They may generate awareness, but they won't necessarily lend support to what a school or district endeavors to accomplish. Schools earn public support by acknowledging and responding to their customers' needs—which far outweighs any newspaper article or television sound bite.

Good News! will introduce you to the Bleikers, but I highly recommend taking their training to grasp the full extent of the role of informed consent, citizen participation, and developing credibility. In addition, many organizations can lend support to a school's community and public relations efforts—for example, the National School Public Relations Society and the Educational Press Association of America. Their publications and Web sites can help educators gauge "hot button" issues and how to handle them (before they become an issue), as well as offer tips on dealing with the media, marketing, advertising, and internal (employee) communications. You'll find a list of resources (contacts) and references at the end of this book.

Finally, good media and community relations is about building trust and relationships, and *Good News!* offers anecdotal information and a course of action that will help you succeed in your efforts. Good luck and best wishes!

Acknowledgments

I owe thanks to everyone, especially Hans and Annemarie Bleiker, who contributed to this book. I relied heavily on interviews, anecdotal stories, and sound personal experiences from the media, schools, and public relations professionals. Many individuals contributed simply by being a part of my everyday work life. I've learned from them the communications tools I carry with me now. Thank you, Corwin Press, for the opportunity!

In particular, I appreciate the help and guidance of the Capital Region BOCES Communications Service staff and Supervisor Judy Cox. The City School District of Albany continues to be one of the best experiences I've ever had professionally; the staff and students are exceptional. It was challenging, educational, and fun. Albany's administrators gave me a great deal of latitude in trying new things. Without the support of former and now retired Superintendent John Bach, Interim Superintendent Eleanor Bartlett, and Assistant Superintendent for Business Affairs Bruce Venter, many ideas and projects may never have seen the light of day.

When attempting to put this book together, I relied primarily on past experiences but also on the expertise of those I trust and who have proved themselves to be sound public relations pros. Washoe County School District Communications Specialist Sonya Gordon was an immense help, as was former BOCES colleague (and friend) Carol Reiser and Sage College's Director of Communications Program and Associate Professor of Communications Kevin Stoner. Former colleague and professional photographer Joe Elario allowed me to use some of his photographs—a few images that only scratch the surface of his phenomenal work with the Albany School District over the years.

The contributions of the following reviewers are also gratefully acknowledged:

Kenneth S. Trump
National School Safety and Security Services
Cleveland, OH

Grant Rich
Assistant Professor, Antioch College
Yellow Springs, OH

Leslie Henrickson
University of California, Los Angeles
Los Angeles, CA

Rocky Killion
Principal, Grimmer Middle School, Lake Central School Corporation
Schererville, IN

Finally, thanks to my parents Don and Bonnie Conners, family members, and dear friends. They believe in me.

—Gail A. Conners

About the Author

Gail A. Conners (BS in television and radio communications, Ithaca College, Ithaca, New York), has served as Public Communications Coordinator for the City of Reno, Nevada, since January 1998. Prior to moving west, she worked as a public information specialist with the Capital Region Board of Cooperative Educational Services in Albany, New York, for 7 years, and as a communications specialist to the City School District of Albany. During her tenure with the district, she created, wrote, and produced *Spirit of Discovery*, a video newsletter airing monthly on local Public Broadcasting Station WMHT. The show covered educational issues as diverse as arts-in-education and school violence. As editor of the district's publications, including its newsletter *Capital Education*, she received more than 50 awards from the Educational Press Association of America, National School Public Relations Association, and New York School Public Relations Association. She has worked as a correspondent to *The Troy Record* and was a member of Press Forward, a group of communicators coordinating the press corps for the Atlanta Committee for the Olympic Games. Her articles have appeared in various publications, including *School Business Affairs.*

1

Using "The Bleiker Lifepreserver" for Positive School-Community Relations

Public Relations is the business of building relationships:
Earning trust, building participation. Once you do these two,
you're able to then motivate behavior.

—Patrick Jackson
Jackson, Jackson, and Wagner
Presentation at Public Relations Society of America Conference; October 20, 1996;
used with permission from Patrick Jackson.

Public relations conjures up various images—from propaganda machines to glitzy "spin doctors." Just mention public relations as part of your overall school strategic plan, and you will likely draw raised eyebrows or chuckles from board members and parents. More often than not, a public relations program is considered a "fringe benefit" that most schools cannot afford. But the truth is that they cannot afford *not* to have one. Although school administrators need to publicize the good news, the public and the media will react even more favorably on how well a school handles a difficult or sensitive situation.

Before launching into a book on getting the best possible news for your school, it is necessary to set the stage by reviewing a set a principles that many government agencies and school districts throughout the country have been using successfully since 1977, when Hans and Annemarie Bleiker (see Photo 1.1) created "The Bleiker Lifepreserver." Their philosophy is key to successful public consent building and public information.

Friends since they attended secondary school together in Wald, Switzerland, the Bleikers have forged a partnership, both marital and business, that has yielded one of the most interesting and important documents created to help build public consent—an essential ingredient in a sound public relations program. Professionally, Hans holds a doctorate in city and regional planning from Massachusetts Institute of Tech-

PHOTO 1.1. Hans and Annemarie Bleiker, Monterey, California
SOURCE: Photograph by Gail A. Conners; used by permission of Hans and Annemarie Bleiker.

nology. Annemarie holds a master's degree in urban anthropology from Brandeis University and worked for years as a planning consultant on socioeconomic issues.

While at MIT in the late 1960s, Hans's graduate studies focused on public-sector decision theory research. He wanted to develop a practical management strategy that allows a public agency to be both responsive and responsible. "Public agencies need to be responsive to their various publics and responsible for the agency's mission," explained Bleiker. "Or agencies need to be responsive or sensitive to the conflicting demands of the potentially affected interests (PAIs) without compromising the agency's mission." What Bleiker accidentally discovered was that many people in public agencies are successful at handling and implementing often difficult situations fraught with problems and public outcry. "These people are implementation geniuses," said Bleiker. So, he began accumulating information and looking for common denominators.

"You see, we as publics want public officials to be responsive, to listen to us and to do want we want them to do, but we also want them to 'get the job done' and accomplish their missions," said Bleiker. According to the Bleikers, therein lies the dilemma—especially with public education. "Accomplishing tough missions, such as educating the young, cannot be accomplished by an administration that also wants to make everybody happy or to have consensus. The problem with trying to make everybody happy is that, earlier or later, some folks are likely to ask for things that interfere with the organization's mission," said Bleiker. "An administration that wants to be so responsive, so sensitive that they are willing to compromise their mission is irresponsible."

On moving to Laramie, Wyoming, Hans became director of the University of Wyoming's graduate planning program. The couple began working together on a program that outlined how government agencies could become more responsible and responsive when interfacing with citizens. "There is an inherent conflict built into the need to be both responsive and responsible. It's not that difficult to be *either* responsible *or* responsive; the challenge is to be both," said Bleiker.

So, the Bleikers began the Citizen Participation Techniques for Public Officials and Other Professionals traveling road show in 1977. During summer recess from the university, the Bleikers took their 3-day course to various cities. The Bleiker Lifepreserver was not intentionally created; it evolved from a set of 60 principles the couple created as part of the 3-day training course in 1977. Since then, the couple has imparted their wisdom to more than 21,000 individuals working in the public sector for the past 22 years. The result: Hundreds of agencies have reaped public recognition and support for complex, often thorny issues that flew in the face of citizen anger, fear, and media attention.

From its inauspicious beginnings as Principle No. 9, The Bleiker Lifepreserver is a system of building informed consent on any issue facing a government agency and its publics. In short, the Lifepreserver approach, when used by a school's administration, holds that the administration must convince all the PAIs, especially those who will be hurt by the proposal in question, of the following:

1. There is a serious problem—or an important opportunity—one that just has to be addressed.

2. You are the right entity to address it; in fact, it would be irresponsible for you, with the mission you have, not to address it.

3. The approach you are taking is reasonable, sensible, and responsible.

4. You are listening; you do care about the costs, the negative effects, and the hardships your actions will cause people.

"Any public sector program or project that doesn't address a problem, or is not perceived to address a serious problem, at least in the United States, is living on borrowed time," said Hans.

"The Lifepreserver is the one principle that kept coming back time and again when we advised people on how to handle the most difficult situations," said Annemarie. "After working on nothing but fiercely contested projects, it became common sense." The Bleikers believe, and have volumes of testimony from former Citizen Participation participants who have used the approach, that unless you can argue convincingly that failure to solve the problem at hand will reduce someone's quality of life significantly, you will have great difficulty convincing the public that the problem at hand is serious.

When districts follow this approach in handling and communicating issues, they build a bank of credibility with their publics by clearly demonstrating accountability. It's a hard pill to swallow for some veteran administrators, however. "We've had people review the principles and The Bleiker Lifepreserver, and they think it's nuts," added Hans. "They immediately ask, 'How can we step forward and discuss the negative stuff? How can we admit that what we're doing might actually hurt someone?' But it works. Good, technical problem solving does not automatically lead to agreement by the public on the course of action chosen."

"Technical analysis, even brilliant technical analysis, usually leads to disagreement, opposition, ultimatums, and posturing, but not agreement," said Hans. The Bleikers' theory is that, in addition to technical problem solving, an agency must clearly state its mission, maintain credibility, make every effort to communicate with and engage citizens in the process, and give them an opportunity to provide input. The results are that even if the public doesn't wholly endorse a project or plan of action, they will grudgingly go along, even if they are hurt by it, because they understand the four points outlined by the Lifepreserver. "Virtually every solution to a complex problem will hurt some interests," said Hans. "By focusing on gaining consent versus consensus, negative situations will not only be minimized, but public agencies become respected and more effective."

School administrators are faced with the same complexities of citizen involvement as their counterparts in government. Your school may be doing a great job, but when it comes to getting a project off the ground, you may find yourself obstructed, stalled, or torpedoed by parents, teachers, board members, or taxpayers. Trying to sell your "feel good news" could fall flat if the public inherently doesn't trust you. "Or worse, people wonder what you're hiding, what your feel-good news is leaving out," said Hans. "Success lies in building a bank of public trust. Trust has to be earned. Feel-good news does not earn trust, it creates suspicion. To build trust demands school administrators communicate in ways that they may consider radical or outrageous."

"Nearly every taxpayer, parent, or potentially affected interest can stop or veto a school's efforts," Hans said. "So, public officials must develop informed consent with their publics in order to solve complex issues. Good communication results in support from those in favor and the grudging willingness of opponents to go along with a course of action they are actually opposed to."

According to the Bleikers, a productive school demonstrates responsiveness and responsibility as part of its overall planning, which includes communication. If safety is an issue, for example, then a school needs to communicate to parents, teachers, and taxpayers what it is doing to address the problem. Therefore, the school is being responsible by developing a plan to address the safety problem. Because the school's planning process, as well as the resulting plan, is bound to step on some people's toes, many individuals will want to make their imprint on the plan.

"That's where the school will have the opportunity to demonstrate its willingness to listen, to be responsive," said Hans. "That, of course, is where the school will come face-to-face with the dilemma of trying to be both responsible and responsive. The school will need to sincerely listen to the input, but not to the point of compromising its mission to solve the safety problems. Some of the input, if incorporated in the plan, will undoubtedly do just that: compromise the safety mission. That input, therefore, will have to be rejected. The challenge, then, is to get the potentially affected interests whose input was rejected to 'grudgingly go along' or to consent to go along."

In 1994, the City School District of Albany, New York, instituted a *School Conduct and Discipline Policy*. The policy was designed to promote responsible student behavior and included a students' bill of rights and responsibilities and disciplinary measures for violations. A brochure was created that outlined the expected behaviors and disciplinary action. In addition, a Safe Schools Committee was created and consisted of school administrators, the district's public information officer, parents, and community leaders. A communications subcommittee was formed to work regularly with PAIs and the media.

At a time when the district was reluctant to deal with the issue of school violence, it demonstrated responsibility by addressing the issue, acknowledging that a problem existed, and publicizing the steps necessary to remedy the situation. It also made every effort to be responsive to concerns expressed by the Albany Public School Teachers Association, as well as by parents and students. As the public information officer, I wrote a two-part series on teen violence in the district's newsletter, *Capital Education* (see Exhibit 1.1).

The articles contained information on the Safe Schools Committee, as well as on conflict-resolution programs and nonviolent crisis intervention sessions for staff. The media were kept abreast of the committee's activities.

Judy Cox has built a mini school communications empire in the Albany, New York, region that has wed Bleiker concepts with school public information programs. A former reporter for the *Rochester Times Union*, Cox later moved to the Albany area where, in 1986, she created and has continued to build the Board of Cooperative Educational Services (BOCES) Communications Service.

EXHIBIT 1.1. *Capital Education*, March/April 1994
SOURCE: City School District of Albany, New York; used by permission.

ALBANY PUBLIC SCHOOLS Capital Education

March/April 1994

Teenage Violence

This is the second article in a series on teenage violence, outlining some of the programs and services currently in existence.

The ever-effervescent Katie Couric, interviewer for NBC's Today Show, was unusually solemn one early morning. Breaking away from her chat with co-anchor Bryant Gumbel, she turned to another story – one not as endearing as the latest actress pitching a movie. She turned to a story that was unfolding in Los Angeles, where teenage ex-gang members were visiting middle and high schoolers, telling their stories of horror and violence. Many of them were in wheelchairs, gunfire had permanently crippled their young lives. Most aren't yet 18 years old. Those in the crowd listened attentively. Many had tears.

While Albany has not witnessed the widespread devastation of teenage street crime found in cities like Los Angeles or New York City, the incidence of violence nationwide has risen. According to the National Center for Health Statistics, gunshots cause 1 in 4 American teenage deaths and is the second leading cause of deaths for Americans between 15 and 34.

The incidence of violence in New York State schools, as reported in a statewide survey in February, has prompted the Board of Regents to suggest to the Legislature and governor that the state should spend $5 million on conflict-resolution programs. The survey was given to more than 12,000 students, teachers, parents and school administrators last year by the State Education Department. Among the more startling statistics were: one in five New York students admitted carrying a weapon to school last year and 10 percent of students admitted

they skipped school at some point because they feared for their safety.

In the City School District of Albany, conflict-resolution and mediation programs have been used, and according to school officials, have largely contributed to reducing potential episodes of violence. In this article, the second and final in the series, programs and services that address the potential for teen violence will be highlighted.

DART

The Center for Alternative Dispute and Resolution (formerly known as the Albany Dispute and Mediation Program) offers a program to school districts throughout the capital region. Commonly known as DART, the program has been at the forefront of conflict-resolution in the City School District of Albany for years.

The first school-oriented program in the area began at Albany High School

in 1987 and currently is in nine schools (Albany High, Hackett and Livingston middle schools, Arbor Hill Elementary, Albany School of Humanities, School 19, Thomas O'Brien Academy of Science and Technology, Montessori Magnet School and School 26).

The center provides training to students and teachers to learn dispute mediation techniques. According to Linda Wistar, Safe Schools Program coordinator, DART provides a means for students to work out their problems without resorting to violence.

"We look at conflict resolution as a process," says Wistar. "It's step-by-step, where teachers and students can negotiate and mediate their relationships with and among each other. The outcome is to ensure the safety for all those involved and to help them make responsible decisions when conflicts occur."

Continued on Pages 3,4

What started with three staff people providing a basic newsletter-writing service for schools has grown to a program that employs 24 people and offers publications, media relations, community relations, grant writing, Web site development, and graphic design. Cox is a full-fledged, dyed-in-the wool Bleiker advocate. In 1992, all members of the BOCES Communications Service were encouraged to attend the Bleikers' Systematic Development of Informed Consent (SDIC) training. Most staff were hired as account executives to local school districts. As a BOCES employee and account executive/public information officer to the City School District of Albany, I participated in the training. As a result of my participation, each account executive incorporated SDIC training and, more specifically, The Bleiker Lifepreserver, into his or her annual communications plans. "I think it's a more honest approach to communicating with the public," said Cox. "It makes more sense. I think we've been successful in helping schools get public support for projects that otherwise would have been torpedoed. People have understood that there was a serious problem, and the school district would have been irresponsible not to handle it. The end result is that schools can accomplish their missions much more effectively when they communicate with the public." She added, "The null alternative to do nothing is not acceptable."

When using The Bleiker Lifepreserver for a particular issue, school administrators need to keep several key points in mind:

- Don't sell the solution, sell the problem. Is it serious? What would happen if you did nothing?

- Keep the school's or district's mission in mind. Are you the right agency to tackle the problem?

- Who is directly affected by the problem? Who may have reason to try to derail or stop your efforts and why?

- Educate and communicate about the problem.

- Review past and current efforts to address the issue. Were you responsible before? Did you listen to all sides of the issue? Did you demonstrate that you cared? Did you fail in your responsibility? If so, state it and make recommendations on how you will change or address it.

Putting Bleiker to Work

The Gunnison Story

One of the most idyllic places to live in the United States is Gunnison, Colorado. Bordering Gunnison National Forest and Crested Butte, and its adjacent ski resort 30 miles north, the Gunnison Watershed RE1J School District was faced with less than idyllic circumstances in 1995.

With less than a year under his belt, newly appointed Superintendent Michael Richardson was looking at a $22 million bond issue for his district. The district is comprised of two main areas—Gunnison and Crested Butte. The larger of the two, Gunnison has nearly 6,000 residents and 1,400 students; Crested Butte has 3,000 residents (including its outlying rural areas) and 350 students. In the early 1960s, Crested Butte lost its high school through consolidation. As a result, students were bused 26 miles one way each day to schools in Gunnison.

"The overall feeling expressed by Crested Butte residents, and deservedly so, was that there was an inequity," said Richardson. "They felt they were continuously getting the short end of the stick." In 1994, a group of Crested Butte parents joined forces to have the school district split. It failed at the polls.

Coming off two sessions of Bleiker training in 1995, one SDIC course, and the more advanced Citizen Participation by Objectives training, Richardson came up with a plan of action built around educating the public. At hand was a bond issue that would include new elementary and middle schools in Gunnison and a new K-12 school in Crested Butte. Richardson and the district hit the ground running.

First, a strategic planning team was assembled that combined those individuals who had worked on the committee to study splitting the district. The 30-member team, as well as newcomers, consisted of administrators, board members, parents, teachers, and two students—one from Gunnison and one from Crested Butte. Beginning in August 1995 and continuing through to the bond issue election in November 1995, a series of public meetings and informal "coffee get-togethers" was held to discuss the issues. Informational brochures were created, and flyers were circulated. The citizenry was given answers to the most pressing questions before they were asked.

"The district's priorities have been guided by our Strategic Plan," said Richardson. "The plan is first and foremost directed at increasing student achievement. We saw that the inequities with Crested Butte and several decaying school buildings limited our ability to accomplish that vision."

The district does not have a public information officer, but brought in project architect Michael Jacoby at every board of education meeting. Jacoby was also present at discussions with the Rotary, Lions, and Kiwanis clubs. The media consistently covered board meetings where the project was part of an ongoing discussion. Letters to the editor were written clarifying misconceptions about the project.

According to *Gunnison Country Times* Associate Editor Paul Wayne Foreman, the district put "a price tag to their plans." A member of the board since 1994 and now RE1J's school board president, Foreman said, "The approach was inclusive. We conducted tours of the facilities and invited the media to see the schools' shortcomings. We finally came up with a plan that the community could afford." Foreman added, "The district instilled a level of trust with the community because they were able to get residents to commit to a level of money without a specific plan."

"Much was accomplished by talking directly with the residents," said Richardson. "We'd meet at a coffee shop and have everybody bring four people."

By applying the Lifepreserver philosophy, negative aspects leading to the bond issue were addressed openly and directly. "We knew that Crested Butte was not getting their fair share," said Richardson. "In fact, four of our five board members live in the greater Gunnison area but totally supported a new facility in Crested Butte."

Armed with Bleiker training, Richardson said the district engaged the negativity that was encountered and never sidestepped or avoided problems. Open discussions were held on why Crested Butte had originally lost its high school. Finally, information was presented that demonstrated the district had grown to the point where it could support another high school program.

"In addition, the buildings were just plain ancient," added Richardson. "There had not been a new school building built in the entire district since 1963." Three of the buildings targeted for demolition were built in 1924, 1927, and 1937. Renovation alone could not address future site expansion, noise, traffic, or congestion problems. In addition, the costs of bringing the buildings up to code proved to be fiscally irresponsible.

The hardships facing the community were increased taxes and a desire by the city to build a new recreation center. Richardson heard such comments as, "It was good enough for me and my father, and it's good enough for my kids." Also, some residents thought the bond was in competition for the same tax dollars as the recreation center.

Board member and Bleiker participant Terry Lowell addressed fiscal concerns in a letter to the editor:

> This bond is for bricks and mortar, not books, furniture, computers or extravagant extras.
> If a home is valued at $100,000, it will cost $98 per year, $8 a month or 26 cents a day.
> Today's interest rates save taxpayers millions in long-term financing costs. It's pay now or pay *more* later. It's time to undertake this critical project.

Richardson sold the problem by using Bleiker's anecdotal theory. "We have one town that's on the fringe of our district, called Pitkin. It's the community with the smallest number of voters, and it had the highest percentage of turnout and highest percentage of 'yes' votes," said Richardson. "One of our board members represents that area, and her point of view is consistent with the residents of that whole area."

The board member's son had been on the freshman basketball team, but because of the existing facility situation, he had to ride a bus 30 miles to get to school by 6 a.m. to practice. No gym space was available after school. His parents had to drive to Gunnison for practice because the bus for that area didn't pick up students until 7 a.m. "The same holds true for members of that team, as well as for the girls' freshman team living in Crested Butte. They had to be driven 28 miles to Gunnison," Richardson added. "With the new school bond, that would never again happen."

In the end, the school bond passed by a vote of 2 to 1. Gunnison now has three full-size gymnasiums with no early morning practice sessions. Crested Butte has a new K-12 building and, according to Richardson, people couldn't be happier.

"The Bleiker philosophy is a part of our board and administrative ethic," he said. "When something comes up, we set out to solve it. We never let the negative get personal, and we acknowledge all points of view." Had the district done nothing, or the null alternative, it would have demonstrated to the public—its shareholders—that it was being irresponsible. "We would have continued to operate with substandard facilities, thus being less than the best we could have been," said Richardson. "Crested Butte probably would have tried again to split off from the rest of the district, and the schism between the two ends of the valley would have widened."

The Fort Collins Story

Gale McGaha Miller knows that, without employing SDIC methods for complex projects affecting many people, "You're asking for trouble." As water quality technical manager for Fort Collins, Colorado, McGaha Miller has been involved in a lengthy biosolids project that could have been fraught with public outcry, but the outcry didn't happen.

McGaha Miller refers to biosolids as "an organic by-product left after cleaning wastewater." The remaining material can be used as fertilizer on agricultural land. "It's higher quality than the topsoil at a gardening store," she said. She did add, however, that people do not like the idea of something that comes from human waste, among other things, as fertilizer.

According to McGaha Miller, Fort Collins realized in the late 1980s that additional land would be needed to recycle their biosolids. The existing facility could only handle one third of the 1,350 dry metric tons per year produced by the city's two wastewater treatment plants. Other concerns were expressed over the possibility of nitrate migration in the shallow groundwater and urban development along the facility's borders.

EXHIBIT 1.2. City of Fort Collins Web Site Home Page
SOURCE: City of Fort Collins; used by permission.

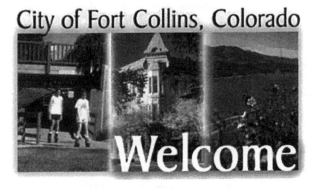

Arts & Culture
Citizen Services
City Hall
Community Planning
Environment
Library
Parks & Recreation
Safety
Transportation
Utilities

Site Evaluation

Often called "The Choice City," Fort Collins offers a unique blend of natural beauty, cultural and recreation opportunities, a strong economic base and diverse employment opportunities. We invite you to explore our site and learn more about the City of Fort Collins.

Last Revision Date: Friday, May 14, 1999 15:09:24
© Copyright 1999 City of Fort Collins

Having had Bleiker training, McGaha Miller, city staff, and engineering consultants reviewed all possible options for the future of long-term biosolids handling. "First, we defined the problem. Then, we made a list of all the potentially affected interests for early input," McGaha Miller explained. "They included our own policymakers, ranchers, citizens, and agricultural, regulatory, and research agencies, in addition to the media. The initial report was circulated among all of them for early input."

Once a report was approved, search for land and citizen participation began. Eventually, staff chose an area removed from urban development where land prices were reasonable. Meadow Springs Ranch, located 22 miles north of Fort Collins near the Wyoming border, was later purchased for this purpose by the city.

From the first investigation in biosolids options through the purchase of Meadow Springs to trial biosolids applications, citizens were part of the overall equation. It was a slow process, and as McGaha Miller said, "Everyone tried to poke holes through the research." The biosolids team was resilient, however. It generated a list of questions and answers about the project and continued to update PAIs regularly.

The staff formed the Citizen's Advisory Committee of ranch neighbors, agencies, and researchers. Results of the latest research were shared, and discussions of opinions and concerns were encouraged. Site tours were conducted, and when new neighbors moved near the ranch, staff met with them and offered to test their drinking water. A newsletter was created and circulated to all PAIs. A separate page was dedicated to the project on the city's Web site (see Exhibits 1.2 and 1.3).

EXHIBIT 1.3. City of Fort Collins Web Site Meadow Springs Ranch Page
SOURCE: City of Fort Collins; used by permission.

News from Meadow Springs Ranch

February 1999

Manager's Message

FIGURE 1
CITY OF FORT COLLINS MEADOW SPRINGS RANCH

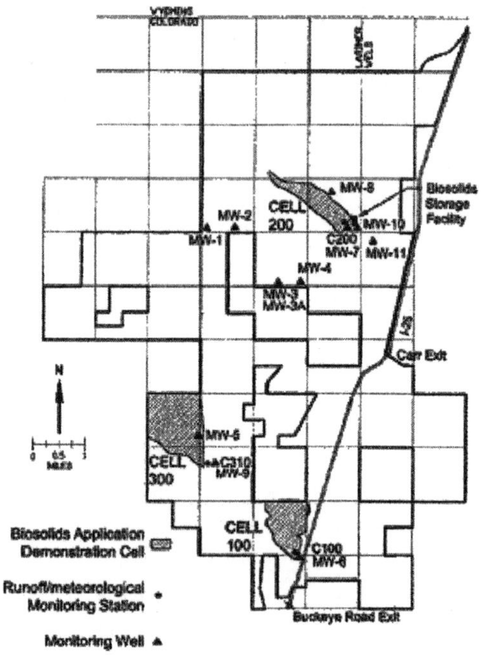

During the last few months, as you might imagine, things at MSR have been a little slow. We have been experiencing a rash of easement requests for wireless communications sites, fiber optic cable, interstate improvements and natural gas lines. To date the City has stayed away from any towers or permanent sites but has been allowing most subsurface requests. It is likely that there will be two easements granted in the North Lonetree pasture this year. Most of the Interstate work has been completed.

The Black footed ferret breeding facility funding has been approved at the federal level. I will be meeting with the engineering group that will be designing the facility later this month. The next step will probably be returning to City Council to approve the land sale that was endorsed by council earlier this year. It is likely that construction could begin this summer if all goes well. If you have specific questions about this facility please don't hesitate to call me at 221 - 6900 and I will try to get answers for you.

Finally, I would like to thank the Diehl ranch for their cooperation and help in fixing some long standing fencing problems in the south west ranch boundaries.

Until next time...

STEVE

Concerns arose over public land located near the research site, which provided well water to citizens. Opposition letters to the editor appeared in local newspapers. "That's when the Citizens Advisory Committee became a useful forum to address these issues," said McGaha Miller.

The committee was also involved in developing a master plan for the site and reviewed the experimental design for each research project. Citizens were kept abreast of all city council meetings in which the project was discussed. The master plan was later approved with few complaints from citizens.

When concerns were voiced, the city listened and responded. "One of the most persistent concerns from citizens was that biosolids would contaminate the aquifer of a well company that supplies drinking water to 2,500 rural customers," said McGaha Miller. The city responded by reviewing hydrogeologic studies to delineate aquifers and to define soil characteristics with the citizens.

McGaha Miller said there was sensitivity to the threatened or endangered species on the ranch. The city generated maps to create boundaries where biosolids would not be used, thereby protecting the inhabitants. The results of all surveys were shared.

The project didn't happen overnight. It took many years from inception and pilot studies to large-scale operation. Midway through the process, the city hosted a field day at the ranch for the media and all interested citizens.

The city staff, much like educators, were faced with citizens who doubted their credibility. "The perception from the farmers was that we were just a bunch of city slickers," she said. The farmers had legitimate concerns, however, and city staff responded. McGaha Miller said that one individual remained a critic. He receives his drinking water from wells surrounding the facility and has read every document created by city staff. Some documents have been modified on the basis of his suggestions, and the city staff perform water quality monitoring to ensure that the aquifer is safe. "It is an ongoing effort to remind him of our organization's mission: that the city listens and cares and is trying to address legitimate concerns. This man may never wholeheartedly support the project, but he does seem to recognize the city's credibility. He has reached that grudging willingness to go along with the project," she said.

The perception from the public, when the city began conducting tours of the facility, was that there would be plenty of "goop." Instead, they saw a smattering of dry material.

During one tour, a staunch critic began complaining about a completely different city program to McGaha Miller. At that point, she knew they had succeeded in gaining credibility with the citizens. "He had lost interest. All his concerns had been addressed," she said.

As public institutions, city governments must address the same issues and concerns as their educational cousins. The goals are the same. Fort Collins was first with the information and examined the impact and hardships on its citizens. The city staff didn't treat concerns as frivolous and incorporated the public into the process. The focus was on consent and not consensus. The city's mission was clearly articulated every step of the way.

"Public agencies usually go into damage control mode when something negative happens, and they want to remain silent," said McGaha Miller. "But when you say, 'Yep, you might get hurt, so let's talk about how it can be minimized,' you gain respect and credibility."

2

Building Credibility and Accountability With the Community

Whether the news media or the school district is seeking credibility, it's a symbiotic relationship.

—KTVN-TV Channel 2 Reno News Director Nancy Cope

Credibility is an asset few companies can afford to be without. In the commercial world, companies can lose millions if the public doesn't believe in or mistrusts their products or missions. Schools and other public agencies can lose valuable support from their communities.

Developing credibility can be likened to a savings bank account. As a school proves accountability to its potentially affected interests (PAIs), whether it's openly discussing test scores, security issues, or graduation rates, the school gains credibility with the public. Each time accountability, responsiveness, and responsibility are shared openly, a school literally deposits public support into a savings account of credibility. Eventually, a school may have to call on that reservoir of goodwill in a tough situation.

Objective 11 of the Bleikers' *Citizen Participation Handbook* (1997) states:

> Credibility, i.e. believability, is essential; it is hard to come by and it is easily lost. We can categorically say that:
>
> - If all interests take your word at face value, you possess an asset—credibility—that is indispensable in searching for and developing informed consent.
>
> - If you do not possess this asset, you need to create it.
>
> - When you possess it, you need to protect and nurture it.

Most everyone working in the public sector accepts these statements as some of the facts of public life. What is less understood is what one can do about it, how one can make deposits into the credibility savings account. Here are the equivalent of deposit slips for that precious savings account:

- Be scrupulously unbiased in the kind of information you release and to whom you release it. Be as frank and open with information that is embarrassing or detrimental to the project as you are with information that is favorable and supportive of the project.

PHOTO 2.1. Chelsea Downs, Reno, Nevada
SOURCE: Photograph by Gail A. Conners; used by permission.

- Be the best, most complete and most reliable source of information. This requires that you not withhold information, even adverse information, because if you do, people can never be sure whether there really is no adverse information about the project or whether you are simply withholding it—covering up.

- Do not classify project information as secret or confidential unless it is absolutely necessary. The existence of confidential information in the hands of a public official smacks of hiding things, cover-ups, lying, deceiving, even corruption and creates a climate of mistrust and suspicion.

SOURCE: Bleiker & Bleiker (1997); used by permission.

In the United States, the public inherently distrusts government and especially those individuals at the top of the policy-making ladder. If someone were to say to you that the board of education or a city government has only the taxpayers' best interests at heart, you would probably respond with, "Yeah, right." This kind of cynical reaction rankles public officials to no end because most of them believe that they really do have the public's best interests at heart. And yet, these rankled public officials are apt to exhibit exactly the same cynical attitude toward other public agencies. Even if the public doesn't support you, now's the time to start building credibility. It is never too late, and it is never too early.

Don't make excuses for past mistakes, but don't be reckless in how you deal with the actions of those who came before you. Even though you do not need to defend what they did, respect the judgment calls they made with the information they had. Be fair. Deal with their actions and decisions the way you hope your successors will deal with your actions and decisions. Deal with the here and now and how to build bridges by demonstrating 100% responsiveness and 100% responsibility. Too often, public agencies operate out of fear of what their constituents will think. The key is to come forward and take responsibility, regardless of the situation. That is how you gain credibility.

The Gunnison Watershed School District RE1J in Gunnison, Colorado, publishes an annual District Accountability Report (see Exhibit 2.1), which outlines the district's annual goals, results, and progress toward the goals. It includes attendance, graduation rates, discipline, community involvement, district assessment, test scores, and a comparative analysis, as well as budget information (see Exhibit 2.2).

In the opening message for the 1996-97 report, School Board President Paul Wayne Foreman invites taxpayers to look at the report with a "critical eye." He writes,

> In keeping with the spirit of the accountability process, we also will look for new ways to involve you in the education of this community's children. After all, being accountable means being accountable to someone: you, the taxpayer, and the parent.
>
> Do not be shy about sharing your views and constructive criticism with the administration or any one or all of the board members. Then realize the invitation to come into the classroom is always open, as is the opportunity to be heard directly and publicly at board meetings. Please, get involved in education.

In demonstrating credibility, the district does not hold back on information. Foreman challenges the PAIs to read it carefully and to contact board members with questions or concerns.

Similar in nature to the Colorado school district, the Mohonasen School District, in Schenectady County, New York, produces an annual District Report Card (see Exhibit 2.3). Debbie Bush-Suflita, a BOCES Communications Service employee and account executive to the district, creates the document, which spells out district findings in clear, concise terms. Based on the New York State Education Department's annual School Report Cards on every public school in the state, Mohonasen's report explains what the data indicates regarding student performance, where the district has had success, and where it needs to work harder (see Exhibit 2.4).

Credibility: Learn to Protect and Enhance It or Learn to Do Without It

Want to destroy your organization's credibility? Here are 12 fast and effective methods for doing just that:

1. Allow someone else to be the **FIRST** source of information.

2. Allow someone else to be the **BEST** source of information.

3. Demonstrate that your critics are **RIGHT** when they claim that you are looking at your project through **ROSE-COLORED** glasses.

4. Deal with people's **LEGITIMATE** concerns as if they were **SILLY OR PHONY**.

5. Pretend to deal with **SILLY** or **PHONY** issues as if you considered them to be **LEGITIMATE** concerns.

6. Be sure to let **OTHERS** bring up the **BIG**, the **CONTROVERSIAL**, the **SENSITIVE**, the **PAINFUL** issues, and then get defensive about them.

(Text continues on page 19)

Gunnison Watershed School District RE1J

1996/1997
District
Accountability
Report

includes accountability reports from:
The Crested Butte Community Schools
Gunnison High School
Gunnison Community School
The Gunnison Valley School
&
The Marble Charter School
District RE1J Accountability:

This is the Accountability Report in full from the year following the bond issue passage and during which the buildings were under construction.

District Accountability Report to the Public for the 1996-1997 school year

Literacy Act Assessment Plan

During the school year the State of Colorado passed House Bill 96-1139 known as the Colorado Basic Literacy Act. The Gunnison School District responded with the implementation of the Benchmark Book assessment program for all first and second grade students. The assessment program uses a series of leveled reading books which the teacher uses with a running record format. 35 out of 235 regular education students were identified as reading below the expected level. Those affected students were all placed on an Individual Literacy Plan (ILP) and will receive the necessary intervention strategies until they are able to read at the expected level.

ITBS, ACT, Plan, Explore

ITBS Percentile Rank by Building—4th Grade

	Blackstock			Crested Butte			District
	M	F	Bldg.	M	F	Bldg.	
Reading	65	62	63	49	66	58	63
Language	54	60	57	41	52	47	55
Mathematics	60	52	57	53	27	39	54
Composite	58	57	58	45	47	46	56
# Students	58	55	113	11	12	23	136

ITBS Longitudinal Analysis (3 years of 3 different classes)

	'94-95	'95-96	'96-97
Reading	67	75	63
Math	64	73	54

Explore Scores by Building—8th Grade

	Ruland			Crested Butte			District	National
	M	F	Bldg.	M	F	Bldg.		
English	14.2	17.4	15.8	18.0	18.3	18.1	16.3	14.0
Mathematics	16.8	17.6	17.2	19.0	16.2	17.9	17.3	14.3
Reading	15.0	19.1	16.9	18.6	18.2	18.3	17.2	13.6
Science	17.5	18.3	17.9	20.1	17.5	19.0	18.1	14.1
Composite	16.0	18.3	17.1	19.0	17.7	18.4	17.4	14.1
#Students	53	50	103	20	12	32	135	-

PLAN Scores—11th Grade

	M	F	District	CO	Nat
English	15.9	18.3	17.2	18.4	16.5
Mathematics	18.0	17.9	17.9	18.7	16.5
Reading	15.5	18.3	17.0	18.0	16.0
Science	18.3	18.7	18.5	19.2	17.0
Composite	17.0	18.5	17.8	18.7	16.6
# Students	46	54	100		

American College Test (ACT) Scores

	M	F	District	CO	Nat
English	19.1	19.8	19.5	20.8	20.3
Math	20.0	18.4	19.2	20.9	20.6
Reading	20.6	21.0	20.8	22.0	21.3
Science	20.9	20.8	20.8	21.8	21.1
Composite	20.3	20.1	20.2	21.5	21.0
# Students	33	38	71		

Longitudinal ACT Score Analysis (3 years of 3 different classes)

	'94-95	'95-96	'96-97
Average Composite Scores			
District	21.0	20.7	20.2
Colorado	21.4	21.4	21.5

Colorado Student Assessment Program (CSAP) Scores—4th Grade

	Unsatisfactory		Partially Proficient		Proficient		Advanced	
	#	%	#	%	#	%	#	%
Reading								
Blackstock	7	6	30	27	68	61	6	5
Crested Butte	1	5	5	23	14	64	1	5
District	8	6	35	26	84	62	7	5
Colorado		11		29		49		8
Writing								
Blackstock	21	21	55	54	25	25	0	0
Crested Butte	2	9	13	59	5	23	1	5
District	23	18	69	55	31	25	1	1
Colorado		22		43		28		3

School District Adopts Model Content Standards

Prior to the State of Colorado mandated January 1997 adoption deadline, the Board of Education has adopted the priority one State of Colorado aligned district content standards in language arts, math, science, and social studies. The staff has been working very hard in these curriculum areas to ensure that instruction aligns with and exceeds the State expectations for all the priority one content area standards.

EXHIBIT 2.3. Mohonasen Central School District Report, Cover

SOURCE: Reprinted with permission of Deborah Bush-Suflita, Communications Coordinator for the Mohonasen Central School District.

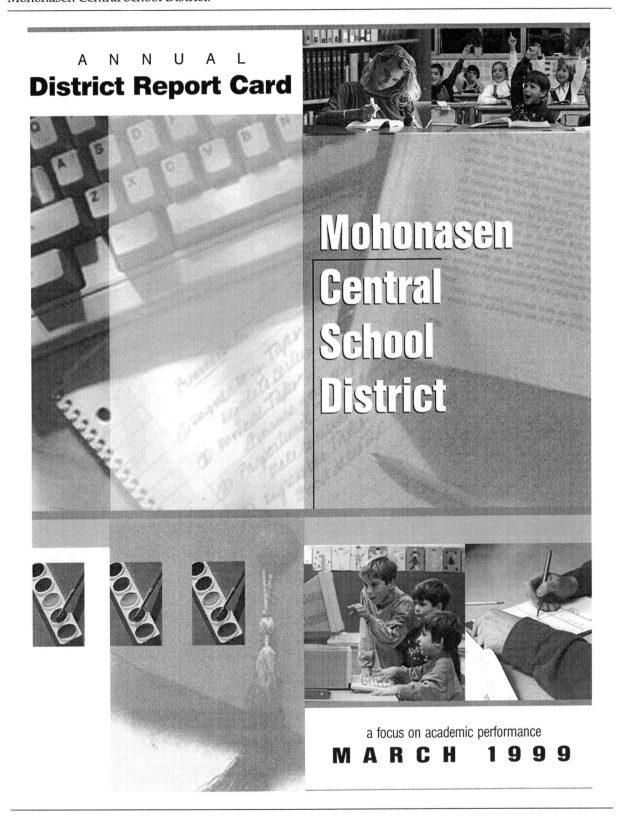

A N N U A L
District Report Card

Mohonasen Central School District

a focus on academic performance
MARCH 1999

EXHIBIT 2.4. Mohonasen Central School District Report, Page 10
SOURCE: Reprinted with permission of Deborah Bush-Suflita, Communications Coordinator for the Mohonasen Central School District.

ANNUAL
District Report Card

Regents Exams

New York State is phasing in its requirement that all public school students take and pass a minimum of five Regents exams to graduate. Although Mohonasen moved to a "Regents for all" *curriculum* beginning with the Class of 2000 (today's Juniors), far too many students still graduate with the less demanding Local Diploma (which the State will eliminate as a choice beginning with the Class of 2005).

Yet all Mohonasen High School students are now enrolled in the more challenging Regents coursework – including those who would otherwise have been in the lower-level "general track" and students needing special education services.

The result is that more students are taking Regents courses and being exposed to a richer curriculum – regardless of whether or not they end up with a Local or Regents Diploma.

The data on this page shows how many students are taking and passing Regents exams. It also shows the percentage of students who are scoring at the "distinction level" by earning scores of 85 or higher.

The chart at right shows test results for all students "theoretically" eligible to take each exam (see definition of Average Grade Enrollment on page 3). No comparative data on the Math 2, Earth Science and Physics exams is available.

Using the junior year English exam as an example, these charts show that 81% of the Mohonasen High School students who took the English Regents last year passed it (chart below). Also, 47% of the entire junior class passed the exam, with 11% of the class scoring 85 or higher (chart at right).

NOTE: Mohonasen High School moved into a more competitive category of "similar schools" for 1998 due to a drop in the number of students eligible for free lunches. 1996 and 1997 similar schools data is reported based on the old "similar schools" category that the high school was in at that time.

1998 Regents Exam Passing and Distinction Rate Comparisons
(BASED ON AVERAGE GRADE ENROLLMENT)

	1996		1997		1998	
	PASSING	85%+	PASSING	85%+	PASSING	85%+
English						
Mohonasen	49%	15%	49%	12%	47%	11%
Similar Schools	55%	16%	61%	18%	76%	25%
All Schools	51%	14%	56%	17%	57%	15%
Foreign Lang.						
Mohonasen	43%	23%	82%	39%	52%	26%
Similar Schools	49%	24%	52%	30%	65%	37%
All Schools	46%	24%	48%	29%	49%	30%
Math 1						
Mohonasen	62%	30%	69%	19%	93%	37%
Similar Schools	58%	29%	49%	20%	61%	30%
All Schools	64%	36%	59%	29%	62%	33%
Math 2						
Mohonasen	48%	19%	39%	18%	47%	16%
Math 3						
Mohonasen	36%	23%	37%	22%	34%	19%
Similar Schools	36%	18%	40%	21%	52%	27%
All Schools	33%	17%	36%	20%	35%	18%
Biology						
Mohonasen	49%	11%	57%	15%	95%	17%
Similar Schools	48%	15%	51%	17%	64%	22%
All Schools	42%	14%	44%	15%	44%	16%
Earth Science						
Mohonasen	49%	11%	58%	16%	40%	12%
Chemistry						
Mohonasen	41%	15%	43%	16%	31%	8%
Similar Schools	34%	11%	37%	13%	48%	17%
All Schools	32%	12%	33%	12%	33%	12%
Physics						
Mohonasen	28%	6%	26%	6%	22%	5%
Global Studies						
Mohonasen	59%	15%	54%	15%	58%	12%
Similar Schools	57%	19%	53%	16%	77%	26%
All Schools	51%	16%	48%	14%	56%	17%
US History & Gov.						
Mohonasen	52%	11%	53%	15%	48%	13%
Similar Schools	54%	19%	52%	17%	73%	26%
All Schools	49%	16%	48%	15%	52%	17%

*Notes: 1. The Regents Exam results shown above are for **all** students, including those with disabilities.*
2. Students who score a grade of 85% or higher on a Regents Exam are performing at the "distinction" level.

Mohonasen Regents Passing Rates
PERCENT PASSING AMONG STUDENTS
ACTUALLY TAKING REGENTS EXAMS, JUNE 1998

English	81%	Earth Science	85%
French	95%	Biology	73%
Spanish	91%	Chemistry	83%
Math 1	65%	Physics	94%
Math 2	58%	Global Studies	71%
Math 3	79%	US History	81%

Mohonasen CENTRAL SCHOOL DISTRICT

7. Be sure you're **UNAVAILABLE** when people, **INCLUDING THE PRESS,** have questions or concerns.

8. **GET DEFENSIVE** about positions and issues that really **DON'T** need defending.

9. **REFUSE** to defend positions and decisions that you **HAVE TO** defend. For example: Be prepared to argue "Yes, in **YOUR** back yard! If that's what you're proposing."

10. Pretend that you know **MORE** than you really know.

11. Pretend that you know **LESS** than you really know.

12. Pretend **NOT** to have the concerns, feelings, emotions, or biases that you **DO** have, or pretend to **HAVE** concerns, feelings, emotions, or biases that, in fact, you **DON'T HAVE.**

SOURCE: Bleiker & Bleiker (1997); used by permission.

School administrators, like all other public officials, always want "good" press; as a result, they are tempted to sugarcoat the information they give to the press. The media are suspicious of sugarcoated coverage; it appears self-serving. Public agencies do not need good press. What they need is coverage that is informative. An informed public leads to an informed public debate. An informed public debate leads to informed political debate, and informed political debate leads to informed political decisions. That's why agencies need informative press rather than good press.

Sound public relations is built on credibility. The media respond well to directness and honesty. When incorporating a responsible approach to communicating, consider that credibility can be instantly lost and difficult to regain. Lying or obscuring the truth is one of the quickest ways to lose credibility, and the media will make sure *everyone* knows.

"I once thought that getting the voters to approve a budget was the bottom line to my job," said Christy Multer, BOCES Public Information Specialist to the Burnt Hills-Ballston Lake Central School District in Saratoga County, New York. "I don't think that anymore. Now I know it's to build and maintain strong credibility with the community. As a school district, everything we do relates to credibility."

In October 1998, voters in the Burnt Hills-Ballston Lake Central School District had to vote on a $13.5 million renovations bond issue. This was a lot of money for a small, 3,300-student school district, but the district was able to use its prior history of passing renovations bond issues every 5 years since 1978.

"The credibility we built with the residents over the previous 20 years made it relatively easy to sell this bond issue even though it was bigger than all the previous referenda combined," said Multer. According to Multer, she, two administrators, and two board of education members laid out a detailed information plan based on credibility to educate the voters (see Exhibit 2.5).

"In the special issue of the *Bulletin* newsletter, we outlined how the voters approved 20 years of referenda. What we were saying was, 'We've been doing this for 20 years, and you can trust us to do these projects on time and within budget,' " said Multer (see Exhibit 2.6).

In 1998, the Washoe County (Nevada) School District faced a situation that could have damaged the school's credibility. The district is the only one in the entire Truckee Meadows area of Nevada, which includes the cities of Reno and Sparks. It has a student population of 52,652.

Elementary school cafeteria workers noticed one day in late February that the Tyson fully cooked chicken product looked slightly undercooked. The Nutrition Services staff were only supposed to "warm up" the product as per instructions. They observed that the meat near the bone was occasionally pink. They

EXHIBIT 2.5. Burnt Hills-Ballston Lake Central Schools Communications Plan, Pages 1 and 2
SOURCE: Burnt Hills-Ballston Lake Central Schools; used by permission.

COMMUNICATIONS PLAN

for the 1998 Renovations Bond Issue
3rd draft—September 4

A. Timeline

July 14	Referendum is discussed at Board meeting
August 11 or 25	Board votes on referendum
Aug. 25, Sept. 8, 22, Oct. 6	Referendum is an agenda item at Board meetings
Tues., Sept. 8	Brief presentation to staff as part of opening day breakfast
Tues., October 13, 5:30, & Wed., October 14, 7:30	Community forums on the referendum, High School library
Wed., October 21	Public vote, 7:00 am-9:00 pm, High School gym

B. Communication Activities

On August 31, Kathleen, Wayne, Bill, Rick, & Christy reviewed previously discussed communications ideas and plans in an attempt to focus and clarify our activities re the bond issue. The following is a summary to date.

Project	Description or Questions	Who and When
Special issue of district newsletter to all households	Send out 8-page, 2-color newsletter similar to Bulletin for last renovations bond issue. Use photos & quotes from members of the Renovations Committee (perhaps Jack Grassmann, Charlie Brown, Melissa Ward, Dennis Bouchard, Paul Borisenko, & Katie Sander?). Will have chart showing tax impact on average home per year ($2 to $19 and back to $2) on front cover. Christy has received newsletter template and graphic items from BOCES designer. Working on drafting prose, Q&A section, taking photos, etc.	Christy In mail by Oct. 1
PTA newsletters	Excellent opportunity to discuss the Bond & incorporate opinions of staff & parents from each building that served on committee. Need to get PTA president's approval and deadline for each building, draft general summary plus projects specific to each building, get comments from building parent and staff committee members.	Kathleen & Wayne
Video	Calls to Charlie Brown have not been returned. A brief, high-quality video would be useful but time is running short.	??
Handouts targeted to various audiences & purposes	Need to have handouts for elementary, middle school, and high school parents. Also handouts summarizing types of projects, cost, and rationale.	Christy & Rick

EXHIBIT 2.5. Continued

Project	Description or Questions	Who and When
Tours of buildings	School principals will incorporate this as they can into their Back to School nights. Also offer tours of High School immediately prior to Homecoming & advertise this in the *Bulletin*. (Note: we should hand out STAR application forms & register voters at Back to School nights too if possible.)	Principals, committee members can help at High School
Community forums on the referendum	In High School library. Summarize projects. Lots of photos. Include tour of High School. Have scheduled 2 forums on different nights & times.	Tues., Oct. 13, 5:30 & Wed., Oct. 14, 7:30
Portable display about the referendum	Photos & descriptions etc. on free-standing display boards of some sort. Could move this from site to site for different meetings. Would be good visual attention getter to use at Community Swim sign-ups, youth athletic sign-ups, craft fair, etc. Include "help yourself" box with handouts.	Will borrow display boards from Power & Light Productions.
Targeted meetings	Have handouts, a display, and/or presentation at: • Business groups • PTA meetings • Back to School nights • Sports booster clubs • Adult Ed. & Community Swim registrations • Youth athletic sign-up sessions	BH-BL BPA = 8:00 am, Wed., Oct. 7 See enclosed calendar.
Web site	Committee report & charts. Can reproduce info from handouts & *Bulletin*. Need to design pages that load quickly. John has begun work on this.	Christy & John Capano
Targeted mailings	Bob McGuire doing mailing to booster clubs *Key Communicators* September issue has been outlined & 1st draft started	Wayne & Christy, Bob McGuire
Neighborhood coffees	Available as requested	

EXHIBIT 2.6. Burnt Hills-Ballston Lake Central Schools Special Issue of the *Bulletin* Newsletter, Page 3
SOURCE: Burnt Hills-Ballston Lake Central Schools; used by permission.

– CONTINUED FROM PAGE 1

would have cost $18.9 million. Through committee discussion, several of the largest initial projects were redesigned for a lower cost. "Every single project was worthwhile," says homemaker and committee member Faith Lesczyznsky. "We haggled and debated. It was difficult to decide which ones should take priority." In the end, the committee recommended 51 projects as the most urgent.

For more information

Copies of the Renovations Committee Report are available at the main office of each school, on the school district's website (www.bhbl.neric.org), or by calling 399-1413. Also, the Board of Education will be holding two **Community Forums on the Renovations Bond Issue** at 5:30 PM on Tuesday, October 13, and at 7:30 PM on Wednesday, October 14, in the High School library.

> *We really scrutinized these projects. It was very difficult to pare them down since they were all well thought out & needed to be done. But the discussion forced us all to think twice and brought out other ways of doing things — half a project or maybe no project in some areas. The process forced the committee to come up with a good product.*

JACK GRASSMANN, RENOVATIONS COMMITTEE CO-CHAIR & GE PROJECT MANAGER

Frequently Asked Questions

How is this different from previous Renovation Bond Issues?

Our school district has used the same basic process to keep its facilities in good shape for the past 20 years: namely, ask a committee of residents and staff to identify the most urgent renovation needs every five years, and seek the voters' approval to borrow money to meet those needs. In fact, by maximizing the use of state aid dollars and by phasing in new debt each year as old debt was paid off, we have been able to fund all 20 years of previous referenda without incurring any additional property taxes.

The most obvious change in this fall's proposed referendum is its size. Issuing $13.5 million in bonds will incur slightly higher levels of debt than we presently have, which will result in the tax increase shown in the chart on page 1. The question voters need to consider is whether current needs and the value of $13.5 million in improvements warrant these additional taxes.

How can over $13 million in school improvements cost the property taxpayer so little?

While property taxes may well continue to increase as the district's annual operating budget increases, issuing renovations bonds and spreading repayment over a number of years can keep the amount of money that renovations add to that increase very small. This is primarily possible because the State will be paying for 84% of these renovations.

Last year state legislators increased the rate of reimbursement for school construction and renovation projects from 74% to 84% because they knew that: (1) many school districts have been unable to maintain their buildings on a planned basis, and (2) most school districts will have difficulty funding all of the instructional and facilities changes required by the new state graduation requirements.

If the Renovations Bond Issue is approved by the voters on October 21, the district will borrow $13,524,243 to renovate its schools over the next five summers (1999 - 2003) and will repay this debt over the next 15 years. The total cost of this borrowing (both principal and interest) is

A tradition of careful planning

BH-BL voters have approved the following 20 years of renovations referenda, which required no new taxes since new debt was added only as old debt was retired.

1978 $870,000 primarily for energy conservation

1983 $1,978,000 for roofing, insulation, and renovation of school shops, auditoriums, gyms & locker rooms

1988 $3,995,946 for 76 projects, including asbestos removal, insulation, roofing & a bus garage addition

1993 $2,649,600 for 47 projects, including roofing, building repair, paving, computers & rebuilding the track

projected to be $18,844,133 over the 15 years. (See chart on next page.)

These estimates are conservative and will be supplemented by interest earned on funds that can be temporarily invested until they are needed to pay for each summer's projects.

immediately pulled the item from the line and substituted another. The district's Nutrition Services stopped serving the product, and the Health Department was contacted.

The Health Department conducted an investigation, which included inspection of the Nutrition Services Center's production facilities. The department found that the district met all requirements in general and in preparing the product. In addition, the department did random inspections at several elementary schools with the full cooperation of the district.

Product food samples and a stool sample from an ill student were forwarded to the state laboratory at the University of Nevada, Reno, for testing. After running tests for salmonella and other harmful microorganisms, the lab determined that the samples tested negative. The one complaint of illness they received from a student was not verified as being related to the incident.

The district took control of the situation by gathering all the facts, working with its Nutrition Services and the local health department, and then issuing a press release that detailed the chronology of the incident and the health department's findings (see Exhibit 2.7). It came forward with information that could potentially have caused parental concern and upheaval. In addition, the district sent letters home to parents at the affected schools, and contacted the media with updated information as often as they could.

"We made sure informational numbers for the schools, Nutrition Services, and the health department were distributed through the media and available to those who asked for them in person or by phone at the school district," explained Sonya Gordon, Communications Specialist, Washoe County School District. "By reacting quickly, our Nutrition Services staff pulled a potential problem food item off the lunch line and made a substitution as soon as possible as a precaution. We thereby averted a possible health risk to our students, which is the district's number one priority. To the public and the media, the school district appeared as prepared and cautious as we should be—and we are. The . . . findings by the health department backed up this fact," she added.

When looking to build credibility into your communications plan or public relations efforts, school staff can follow these guidelines, as written by the BOCES Communications Service (Cox, n.d.):

- Use your newsletter to discuss news, and not only good news. School districts have problems. Talk about those problems and what the district is doing to resolve them. Believe it or not, the public is very forgiving of frailties, particularly when they see that you recognize those frailties and are trying to do something about them.

- If you are going to use any opinion in a newsletter story, make sure you back it up with facts. For example, if you describe a teacher contract settlement as fair, show exactly how much the raises are and how they compare to other districts. If you describe a sports program as being good for students, show how many students are involved and what value they receive from that participation. People can argue with opinion, but it's hard for them to dispute or dismiss the facts.

- Don't be afraid of controversy. If the community is talking about it, you should be writing about it. Many times bringing the issues right out on the table diffuses the controversy. Here again, you should always lean more heavily towards facts than opinion.

- Become sensitive to what people out in the schools and in the community are saying and what they are grumbling about. This will help you avoid writing anything that will be easily dismissed as lies. Also, be willing to question district officials closely. They may not be lying to you, but they may be afraid to speak the entire truth. You are doing them

(Text continues on page 26)

NEWS RELEASE

||||||||||||||||||||||||||||||||||||||||||||||||||||||||||||||||||||||||||||||||||||||||||||||||||||||

Date: March 13, 1998

Washoe County School District
425 East Ninth Street • Reno, NV 89520
Communications/Information Office
(702) 348-0371 • (FAX) 348-0397

Contact: Steve Mulvenon/Sonya Gordon

WASHOE COUNTY HEALTH DEPARTMENT COMPLIMENTS NUTRITION SERVICES AFTER 'CHICKEN' INVESTIGATION
No Link Discovered Between Sole Student Complaint And Chicken

RENO-SPARKS -- The results of the Washoe County District Health Department's investigation of the school district Nutrition Services Division's handling of what appeared to be slightly underdone chicken are in, and they're something for the school district to crow about.

In late February, some elementary schools' cafeteria workers discovered what appeared to be slightly underdone chicken had been prepared at lunch time. The pre-cooked chicken product, Tyson Foods' Fully Cooked Chicken Products, is warmed in a convectional oven at 375 degrees for 20 to 25 minutes, according to instructions on the box.

Many schools pulled the item from the line and substituted it for another when they discovered the meat near the bone occasionally was still pink. Tyson Foods is investigating the product sent to WCSD, and Nutrition Services ceased serving that particular product.

The Health Department reported "the investigators were impressed with the demonstrable knowledge of good food sanitation practices and procedures at the Washoe County School District (WCSD)."

On February 20, one Foodborne Illness Complaint implicating the chicken was received by the Health Department regarding a student, and the Health Department's public health environmentalists conducted a Foodborne Illness Investigation of the Nutrition Services Center production facilities.

It was noted at the time, according to the Health Department report, "that the employees do not touch food products with bare hands at any stage of pre-processing and/or repackaging. All refrigeration units were found in good repair, and all units showed temperatures within legal ranges. Temperature verification logs were found throughout the establishment at key locations ... . All thawing of potentially hazardous food products occurs under refrigeration."

On that same day, the environmentalists also did a random inspection of the Bernice Mathews Elementary School kitchen to determine how the product is "typically" handled and processed in satellite locations.

-MORE-

EXHIBIT 2.7. Continued

WASHOE COUNTY SCHOOLS -- CHICKEN REPORT/2

At Mathews Elementary, according to the report, the "operator of the kitchen demonstrated good knowledge of sanitary food-handling practices. Documentation to verify final cooking temperatures (CCP) was found current and on-site. Implicated food products at this site are documented to have been cooked to internal temperature in excess of 163 degrees farenheit, though school district product specifications designate a minimum internal cooking temperature of 145 degrees farenheit for this product." In addition, the inspectors found "hot holding equipment appeared to be operating properly and capable of holding potentially hazardous food items at required temperatures."

Health Department staff also collected four samples of what appeared to be slightly undercooked Tyson chicken product on February 23, delivering them and a stool sample from the ill student to the State Laboratory at the University of Nevada, Reno. The district Health Department requested the laboratory run the sample to detect the presence of Salmonella, Bacillus cereus, Clostridium perfringens and Campylobacter microorganisms. On March 2, the laboratory reported that the "food samples tested negative for the presence of Salmonella, Bacillus cereus, Clostridium perfringens and Campylobacter microorganisms. The stool sample collected by the District Health Department tested negative for signs of foodborne related illness."

Therefore, the findings of the investigation do not support a causal relationship between the illness reported and the suspect food product examined. According to the report, "This conclusion is drawn from the apparent absence of any complaints other than the single incident investigated by the Health Authority, the negative findings of the representative laboratory evidence and the efficacy of food sanitation measures as instituted by the Washoe County School District and verified by the investigators."

-30-

no favors by merely parroting what they say, particularly if it is going to cause the public to turn away in disgust and disbelief.

- Be timely with your communications. People in the community should learn about new developments as they occur. They also should learn about problems as soon as the district identifies them. Plus, they should hear the news from the district, not from other sources. If you only have a quarterly newsletter and information needs to be released immediately, create a short flier or letter that deals directly with the issue and send it home with students. Today, of course, the thing to do is create a Web site, which is constantly updated, so parents as well as staff can keep up to date on information.

Remember that school districts work on the reverse pyramid concept. As far as the public is concerned, the least credible sources of information are the people at the top. You can write stories until you're blue in the face about how economically the school district is being run, but if the teachers or janitors or bus drivers are talking out in the community about the incredible amount of waste they see, then you're dead.

Most important of all, have faith in the public—both internal and external. Don't be afraid to discuss any topic or share any kind of information with them. Being open will sometimes get you into trouble, at least temporarily, but not nearly as much trouble as you would if your public feels that you are withholding things they have the right to know about. In other words, some people will criticize the district once certain things are shared with them. But in the end, openness is the only way to develop the trust bank. These very same people who criticize you will also come to respect you.

SOURCE: Cox (n.d.); used by permission.

In autumn 1997, the City School District of Albany (New York) established school safety initiatives. The result was the formation of Safe and Friendly Environment (SAFE) to ensure a violence-free environment for all students. "At the same time, there was much media speculation about school violence," said David Albert, District Public Information Specialist. "Even prior to the Littleton, Colorado, event, the one single topic that had generated the most media requests was school safety."

Within months of SAFE's birth, District Superintendent Lonnie Palmer participated in an editorial board with the *Times Union* newspaper. Questions were posed about what steps the district was taking to make schools safe. Palmer replied that one consideration was to install video cameras. Although no cameras were installed at that time, the idea gained momentum. By December 1997, surveillance cameras were installed at Albany High School, as well as at Hackett and Livingston Middle Schools.

The district's actions could have been viewed as excessive, or as Albert said, "People could perceive that the schools are filled with criminal activity, and that's not necessarily the case. We were already taking steps to create a safer environment, and we wanted to be up front about everything we were doing."

With the SAFE committee, the district first reviewed everything it was already doing to prevent violence. Much had been created that dealt with punitive actions for discipline violations, but little was on the books that dealt with preventative measures. As a result, the district not only decided to install surveillance cameras but also banned such items as pagers, beepers, cell phones, and overcoats, which could conceal weapons.

The media began calling even before the cameras were completely installed. "One station even wanted to do a poll as to whether cameras were a good or bad idea," said Albert. "Finally, we decided to hold a press conference and invite everyone" (see Exhibit 2.8).

Joining the district at the press conference were Albany Police Chief Kevin Tuffey, Mayor Gerald Jennings, and SAFE committee members, as well as students and parents. Following the conference, all in attendance were invited to tour the facility and witness the cameras in action.

"We made students available to answer questions because some wondered whether the district's decision to install cameras was an invasion of privacy," said Albert. "We came forward with all information because we wanted to reassure parents that the district was being proactive and that the students are safe at school." Albert said that he has witnessed other districts downplay broadcasting such actions because it would "reflect poorly on them. But, by hiding it, by not being forthcoming, the perception is that there's something going on in a district that they need to keep on top of. It's not a good way to build credibility. The more a school or district tries to do something without people knowing, the more vigilant the public will be in trying to keep an eye on you," he said.

When dealing with the media, credibility is earned by

- Being direct and honest

- Responding quickly and being mindful of deadlines

- Admitting mistakes and explaining what you'll do to address them

- Having accurate information

- Saying "thank you" to the reporter and/or assignment editor when she or he has done a good job

- Not playing favorites

- Not frequently calling with frivolous requests (e.g., correcting minor mistakes)

- Not berating them for only covering perceived negative stories

"Whether the news media or the school district is seeking credibility, it's a symbiotic relationship," said KTVN-TV Channel 2 Reno News Director Nancy Cope. "We depend on each other, so we both need to get the facts straight, return phone calls, understand how each other works, be knowledgeable and available."

EXHIBIT 2.8. City School District of Albany Press Release on "SAFE," December 10, 1997
SOURCE: City School District of Albany; used by permission.

News from the City School District of Albany

Academy Park, Albany NY 12207
Contact: David Albert, Public Information
(518) 462-7228

December 10, 1997

<u>For Immediate Release</u>

Albany schools taking steps to remain "SAFE"

Comprehensive "<u>S</u>afe <u>A</u>nd <u>F</u>riendly <u>E</u>nvironment" package includes alternative education, video cameras and improved security.

The City School District of Albany today announced the introduction of comprehensive school safety measures at the middle- and high-school levels. The implementation of these measures adds Albany to the growing number of local school districts, including Bethlehem and Voorheesville, which have expanded their security initiatives.

"The Albany Board of Education set the priority of having the safest schools in the area. Now we are seeing great results," says school board Vice President Ben Conboy, who sponsored the original safe schools resolution last spring.

"Above all else, parents want their children to be safe in school. In Albany, we take that concern very seriously," adds Superintendent Lonnie Palmer, who dubbed the comprehensive school safety program with the acronym "SAFE" (<u>S</u>afe <u>A</u>nd <u>F</u>riendly <u>E</u>nvironment). Palmer stresses that the plan contains proactive measures designed to ensure that the schools remain safe. Components of the plan include:

+ The formation of a school district security team, composed of a security director, four security officers and hall monitors. One security officer each will be stationed at Albany High School, Harriet Gibbons High School, Hackett Middle School and Philip Livingston Magnet Academy.

+ The creation of more alternative educational environments for students who have behavioral or academic problems. The district is working with community based organizations such as the Urban League to create these alternative schools, which supplement the existing programs at School 21, Harriet Gibbons High School and the "TOPS" Program.

+ The installation of video surveillance cameras at Albany High School.

+ The issuance of photo identification cards for all students at Albany High School. Students on school grounds must carry their cards with them at all times.

-more-

28

EXHIBIT 2.8. Continued

Comprehensive "SAFE" Initiative   Page 2

+   A prohibition on wearing most overcoats and hats and using electronic devices (beepers, radios, etc.) inside school district buildings.

Part of the comprehensive initiative includes alternative educational programming for disruptive students. "Education does not come in the 'one-size-fits-all variety,'" says Palmer. "Our security package would not be complete without new and innovative educational placements for students who have not been successful in the traditional school environment."

"We will not allow disruptive students to usurp valuable class time that should be devoted to instruction. What we will do is provide them with quality teachers and challenging assignments in alternative educational environments," adds Palmer, pointing out that some students thrive academically and personally when they enter an alternative school, which often provides them with smaller classes, more individual attention from the teacher and fewer distractions.

School officials pledged to protect the rights and privacy of its students, teachers and staff. Albany High School Principal Dr. Willard Washburn says, "These new organizational design and security measures will help us deter individuals from violating the district's safe schools policy and code of conduct. At the same time, we remain committed to building a spirited school community in which academic and extracurricular pursuits create a positive atmosphere."

-30-

3

Developing a
Communications Plan

Before the media ever call your school or district, one of the most important documents you can create is a communications plan for the school year. Schools are businesses, and most businesses have communications plans built around the company's mission and strategic plan. A plan provides the school and administration with an outline that helps focus communications efforts by addressing the goals and priorities of the state education department, board of education, and district or school for the year. A plan that includes measurable outcomes can also demonstrate that a school is being responsive and responsible to its shareholders.

Plans need not be lengthy, time-consuming pieces of work. Rather, they should reflect the district's and/or school's goals, the strategies to be used, and the process in which those goals will be carried out. An overall plan helps deliver the school's mission by using a variety of communications tools.

One source for prioritizing goals, aside from a board of education, is a district or school's communications committee. Comprised of parents, teachers, administrators, and key communicators from the community, a communications committee may already exist that can assess the school's assets and deficits in relaying information. In short, what does the community want to know, and how should you deliver the information?

"A plan helps focus what you want to do for the year," said Deborah Bush-Suflita, BOCES Communications Service employee and account executive to the Rotterdam Mohonasen Central School District in Schenectady County, New York. "But once it's written, it's good to go back and review it from time to time. Because even though you may make a conscious decision to do one thing, any variety of circumstances or emergencies will come up during the year which could derail your plan."

In drafting the 1998-99 plan, Bush-Suflita reviewed the district's goals, made a list of other events/priorities for the upcoming year, and combined the two. "I tried to merge it together into a plan that could accommodate a full-time position," she said. Then she discussed the plan with School District Superintendent Audrey Farnsworth, who added items to the list.

Bush-Suflita also writes quarterly reports in which she summarizes her communications efforts to date. The reports outline activities that support the annual plan, as well as those not anticipated. It is then shared with the superintendent and board of education to keep them abreast of public information efforts.

In writing her communications plan for the 1998-99 school year, Bush-Suflita used the New York State Education Department's initiatives as a guideline for the Mohonasen plan. "The New York State Education Department is raising educational standards and changing graduation requirements," she explained.

PHOTO 3.1. Montessori Magnet School Student Colin Ross, Albany, New York
SOURCE: Photograph by Joe Elario; used by permission.

PHOTO 3.2. Reno, Nevada, Libby Booth Elementary School Students Shane Vasquez (left) and Ivy Mujica (right)
SOURCE: Photograph by Gail A. Conners; used by permission.

"Consequently, one of Mohonasen's goals for the 1998-99 school year is to continue working hard to raise standards and improve results for all children."

That goal is reflected in the communications plan, which stipulates that the school district will produce a comprehensive report on all its schools, publish the data in its newsletter, and work with the media. Much of the district's communications effort has served to educate the public on the state's new requirements.

Detailed and concise, Exhibit 3.1 is a good example of a thorough communications plan from the Rotterdam Mohonasen Central School District. It includes goals, strategies, and a planned course of action for the entire year.

EXHIBIT 3.1. Rotterdam Mohonasen 1998-99 Communications Plan

SOURCE: Reprinted with permission of Deborah Bush-Suflita, Communications Coordinator for the Mohonasen Central School District, Rotterdam, NY.

M·O·H·O·N·A·S·E·N 1998-99 Communications Plan · DRAFT

Developed by the Capital Region BOCES Communications Service · 9/98

District Goals	Communication Needs	Communication Projects
INCREASE COMMUNICATION WITH STUDENTS, PARENTS AND THE PUBLIC. SPECIFICALLY: • *Increase information to parents and students regarding learning standards, graduation requirements and expectations.* • *Sustain the Goals 2000 initiative.* • *Identify a liaison to study legislative issues.* **Also:** • *Continue to expand the number of school-to-career pathways.*	Mohonasen recognizes the key role that parents play in helping students come to school motivated and ready to learn. This role begins in infancy and continues right through high school. More parental involvement has been identified as a recurring need in the district's efforts to restructure the entire educational system to improve student results. To help parents become more actively involved in helping their children succeed in school, Mohonasen would like to: • Increase information to parents and students regarding learning standards, new graduation requirements and expectations in order to help parents understand WHY there is a need for higher standards and HOW restructuring will impact their children. • Provide all parents with support and information on how to help their children succeed in school. • Increase parent attendance at workshops and participation in school programs/events. • Inform parents about legislative issues that impact our schools and the school budget.	To help the district reach this goal, the Communications Service will undertake the following projects in 1998-99: 1. **CREATE A 24-PAGE CALENDAR AROUND THE THEME OF "SCHOOL TO CAREERS"** that builds parents and community understanding and support for Mohonasen's school-to-careers programming. Through quotes, photos and articles, the calendar will build a case for why education needs to be both rigorous and relevant. It will also show the many components of Mohonasen's ever expanding school-to-careers system. As always, the calendar will also be an important tool for informing the entire community about dates for school events, workshops and other activities throughout the year. 2. **SERVE AS A COMMUNICATIONS CONSULTANT FOR DISTRICT PROGRAMS/INITIATIVES TARGETING PARENT INVOLVEMENT.** Examples include newsletter stories, press releases and/or publications work regarding: • The EPIC Parent-to-Parent Support Program • The 1000 Book Child Project • Goals 2000 initiatives • Parent workshops on study skills/helping students handle homework effectively 3. **CONSULT WITH BOCES TEAM MEMBER ON DEVELOPMENT & DESIGN OF FACT SHEETS ON NEW GRADUATION REQUIREMENTS FOR EACH GRADE** beginning with this year's 6th-grade (class of 2005 and beyond). 4. **WRITE AND DESIGN A CAREER PATHWAYS BROCHURE** that provides an overview of Mohonasen's pathways for students, parents and local businesses. 5. **LIAISON WITH BOCES GRAPHICS DEPT. TO UPDATE THE 1999-2000 HIGH SCHOOL COURSE GUIDE/ HANDBOOK** for parents and students. • Cover/templates redesigned for black and white reproduction? *NOTE: EDITING/CORRECTIONS NEED TO BE HIGHLIGHTED BY THE APPROPRIATE HS STAFF AND WORKED OUT DIRECTLY WITH BOCES GRAPHIC SUPPORT STAFF.* – GOAL #1 CONTINUED ON NEXT PAGE –

Page 1 of 2
Goal #1

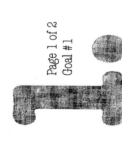

33

EXHIBIT 3.1. Continued

M·O·H·O·N·A·S·E·N 1998-99 Communications Plan · DRAFT

Developed by the Capital Region BOCES Communications Service · 9/98

District Goals	Communication Needs	Communication Projects
INCREASE COMMUNICATION WITH STUDENTS, PARENTS AND THE PUBLIC. SPECIFICALLY: • *Increase information to parents and students regarding learning standards, graduation requirements and expectations.* • *Sustain the Goals 2000 initiative.* • *Identify a liaison to study legislative issues.* *Also:* • *Continue to expand the number of school-to-career pathways.*		6. **(VIA BOCES COMMUNICATIONS TEAM) PRODUCE AN INFORMATIONAL BROCHURE ON THE STAR PROGRAM** that is updated for the next phase of that program and fully explains application deadlines, etc. 7. **CREATE "WE'RE LISTENING" FORM** for use in gathering written feedback from parents and others. The forms will be published in all newsletters beginning with the October issue and will be available at all board of education meetings. 8. **SERVE ON GOALS 2000 PLANNING COMMITTEE** to plan year 2000 events/publicity. 9. **WRITE RELATED STORIES IN THE DISTRICT NEWSLETTER.** Story ideas include: • Odyssey of the Mind teams/competition • The new criteria for placement into honors courses to assure participation is available to all students who want to be challenged. (Report expected in January) • The new part 100 regulations (expected in November) from the Board of Regents, the impact these will have on kids and the budget implications of these regulations, if any. • Spotlight students achievement in the annual year-end awards issue.

Page 2 of 2
Goal #1

34

EXHIBIT 3.1. Continued

M·O·H·O·N·A·S·E·N 1998-99 Communications Plan · DRAFT

Developed by the Capital Region BOCES Communications Service · 9/98

District Goals	Communication Needs	Communication Projects
CONTINUE TO SHAPE THE EDUCATIONAL SYSTEM K-12 TO OBTAIN STUDENT ACHIEVEMENT LEVELS THAT ARE COMPARABLE TO SIMILAR DISTRICTS IN THE REGION AND ACROSS THE STATE WITH 90% OF OUR STUDENTS ABOVE THE STATEWIDE REFERENCE POINT ON STATE ASSESS-MENTS AND THE PASSING SCORE ON REGENTS EXAMINATIONS.	CLOSELY RELATED TO GOAL #1, Mohonasen is working hard to raise standards and improve results for all children. Significant changes are taking place in virtually every aspect of Mohonasen's curriculum, instruction, assessment and reporting practices. A lot more is being asked of teachers, parents and students as the district raises expectations and toughens both testing and graduation require-ments. Now more than ever, good communication is essential to Mohonasen's efforts to improve results. The district recognizes the need to communicate regularly about the reasons for higher standards – and what they will mean for students, teachers, parents and taxpayers. Rapid improvements in student achievement will be virtually impossible without the understand-ing and consent of the community Mohonasen serves.	To help the district reach this goal, the Communications Service will undertake the following projects in 1998-99: 1. **PRODUCE A COMPREHENSIVE REPORT CARD ON OUR SCHOOLS** WITH A SPECIAL SECTION ON ENGLISH/LANGUAGE ARTS REPORTED. The special section on English/Language Arts would report test score results over time (K-12) and contain a detailed report on all the things the district has done over the last five years to improve student literacy and align curriculum with the new standards. Test score data will be reported within the context of the district's educational goals and priorities. • Work with the superintendent of schools and building principals to analyze data and develop key message points that summarize areas where test scores are strong, where they are not and what the district is doing to make improvements in key areas. • Summarize test data in a story in the February(?) district newsletter. • Consult on report card presentations at Board/PTO/PTSO meetings. • Work with local reporters as appropriate to ensure accurate coverage of data. • Post the report card data on the district web site. 2. **USE THE DISTRICT NEWSLETTER** as a vehicle to showcase programs and initiatives that are helping to move the district forward and improve student results on new and existing assessments. Story ideas include: • How technology is being used as a tool to achieve higher standards. • The new assessments and the graduation requirements, the phase-in schedule and what it means for kids. • The Tolcott Mountain grant and the use of web TV in student homes. • Collaborative ventures with SUNY Albany researchers/professors 3. **RESEARCH AND WRITE UP OVERVIEW OF LITERACY INITIATIVES AT MOHONASEN** AS PART OF EFFORT TO INTEREST LOCAL MEDIA IN DOING A REGIONAL SERIES ON THE WAYS CAPTIAL REGION SCHOOLS ARE WORKING TO BOOST STUDENT LITERACY.

EXHIBIT 3.1. Continued

M·O·H·O·N·A·S·E·N 1998-99 Communications Plan · DRAFT

Developed by the Capital Region BOCES Communications Service · 9/98

District Goals	Communication Needs	Communication Projects
DEVELOP A PLAN FOR THE EFFECTIVE OPERATION OF THE MOHONASEN WEB SITE.	The district has received numerous requests from residents and staff for expanded information on the Mohonasen web site. While the district has no clear measure of how many residents are currently on-line, two things are clear: the number of on-line subscribers is rapidly growing around the country and Web communication is clearly not a passing fad. The Mohonasen web site will grow in importance as a communications tool in the years ahead as today's "Generation Xers" (who cut their teeth on this technology) become the parents of our elementary school children. The site also has enormous potential as a tool to promote on-line/at-home learning — for both children and adults. This medium will not replace print in the near future, but it certainly will become AS important. The Web is *immediate* (information can be changed hourly); *cost-effective* (no printing or mailing costs) and *interactive* (inviting immediate feedback). Its potential has only begun to be tapped.	To help the district reach this goal, the Communications Service will undertake the following projects in 1998-99. 1. **MERGE THE TWO EXISTING WEB SITES.** [www.mohonasen.org and www.global2000.net/school/mohonasen] The two web sites will be merged and housed together on the district server under the URL of www.mohonasen.org with the district-level site being the home page. Create a "We've moved" page at the Global 2000 address with a direct link to the new address and maintain that site for one year. 2. **EXPLORE THE DEVELOPMENT OF A DATABASE DRIVEN WEBSITE**. 3. **MAINTAIN/UPDATE THE *"WHAT'S NEW?"* PAGE ON A WEEKLY BASIS.** This includes information briefs for each of the following five categories: • *In the News* – pick one or two items to publicize each week. • *Board of Education* – Publicize meetings in advance and pick one or two agenda items and/or board actions to publicize every other week. • *Special Events and Meetings* – Highlight a few events each week and any date changes that occur from the printed calendar. (Also add to on-line calendar/see below) • *Web Pick of the Month* – Pick one or two sites to feature with direct links. (Also create a link to a page of just former web picks.) • *New on Our School Pages* – Pick one or two building level pages to feature. 4. **UPDATE CONTENT ON THE FOLLOWING EXISTING PAGES:** ❑ *FAST FAQS* • *Budget FAQs* – First update with information on existing 1998-99 budget and later (April/May) with information on proposed 1999-00 budget • *Enrollment FAQs* – Update using 10/1/98 figures. • *Community FAQs* – Update section on budget.

Page 1 of 4
Goal #3

– GOAL #3 CONTINUED ON NEXT PAGE –

EXHIBIT 3.1. Continued

M · O · H · O · N · A · S · E · N 1998-99 Communications Plan · DRAFT

Developed by the Capital Region BOCES Communications Service · 9/98

District Goals	Communication Needs	Communication Projects

District Goals

DEVELOP A PLAN FOR THE EFFECTIVE OPERATION OF THE MOHONASEN WEB SITE.

Communication Projects

4. UPDATE CONTENT ON THE FOLLOWING EXISTING PAGES – CONTINUED

☐ *CALENDAR ON-LINE PAGE*
 • Make ongoing updates to the on-line calendar and notify all appropriate staff to send me updates thru the web or thru e-mail when dates are changed or added.

☐ *VISIT OUR SCHOOLS*
 • *Ten Things to Check out at Bradt* – Rewrite and add Bradt photo(s)
 • *Ten Things to Check out at Pinewood* – Rewrite and add Pinewood photo(s)
 • *Ten Things to Check out at Draper* – Rewrite and add Draper photo(s)
 • *Ten Things to Check out at Mohonasen HS* – Rewrite and add Mohonasen photo(s)

☐ *LINKS PAGE*
 • *Web Resources* – Update the extensive links section which includes fixing bad links and adding new links as appropriate

☐ *NEWSLETTERS ON-LINE PAGE*
 • Post PDF files with links as new editions of the newsletters are published.

☐ *ANNUAL SCHOOL REPORT CARDS*
 • Put 1997-98 school report cards on-line when they become available.

5. **IMPROVE THE DESIGN OF THE *"DIRECTORY"* PAGE** so that it better prioritizes/accommodates all the pages on this growing site. Also provide direct graphical links to each school straight from the directory.

6. **IMPROVE THE *"WHAT DO YOU THINK?"* PAGE** to gather relevant information in a way that is easier to understand.
 • This will involve getting a technician to write a new cgi script that works on the Mohonasen/NERIC server (to replace the old Global 2000 cgi script)
 • Revise content/questions within this page to make them more open-ended and easier to understand on the receiving end.

 – GOAL #3 CONTINUED ON NEXT PAGE –

Page 2 of 4
Goal #3

37

EXHIBIT 3.1. Continued

M·O·H·O·N·A·S·E·N 1998-99 Communications Plan · DRAFT

Developed by the Capital Region BOCES Communications Service · 9/98

District Goals	Communication Needs	Communication Projects
DEVELOP A PLAN FOR THE EFFECTIVE OPERATION OF THE MOHONASEN WEB SITE.		7. **REGISTER THE SITE WITH MAJOR INTERNET SEARCH ENGINES.** 8. **DEVELOP THE *CONSTRUCTION PROJECT UPDATE* PAGE(S).** This page will essentially be a photo gallery depicting the stages of the $20 million capital project, time-lines for completion, etc. It will involve: • Creating a photographic "history" of the $20.1 million construction project from ground breaking through various stages of completion. Project Manager Jeff West will assist by taking many of the photos. • Writing content for the pages (scope of the project, time line for completion, etc.) and captions for photos as they are added. 9. **MISCELANEOUS DESIGN/TECHNICAL ADJUSTMENTS** needed to existing pages: • Fix the PDF files for the *Annual School Report Cards* page. (This will require going back into original print files.) • Try to improve the clarity of type in the PDF files for the newsletters and report cards. • Add a counter to record the number of hits. • Set up capability for posting school closing information from home. • Fix headers on What's New page so they appear at top of block (or repeat thruout) 10. **WORK WITH MOHONASEN ADMINISTRATORS/STAFF TO DEVELOP AND IMPLEMENT GUIDE-LINES AND POLICIES FOR BUILDING-LEVEL WEB PAGES** including: • Staff guidelines for content – what's appropriate and what's not appropriate. • **DEVELOP STANDARD PAGE TEMPLATES (IN MICROSOFT WORD)** for use by teachers and other building-level staff. These pages will include navigational buttons and lend a consistent and professional look to all teacher web pages. • Policies for proofreading – content and links • Policies for keeping pages updated. • Policies for oversight of district-level vs. building-level pages. – GOAL #3 CONTINUED ON NEXT PAGE –

Page 3 of 4
Goal #3

EXHIBIT 3.1. Continued

M·O·H·O·N·A·S·E·N 1998-99 Communications Plan · DRAFT

Developed by the Capital Region BOCES Communications Service · 9/98

District Goals	Communication Needs	Communication Projects
DEVELOP A PLAN FOR THE EFFECTIVE OPERATION OF THE MOHONASEN WEB SITE.		11. **WORK WITH STUDENT INTERN TO CREATE *"MOHONASEN MUSIC"* PAGES** that explain the band, orchestra and chorus programs, provide a vehicle for more timely information on competitions, list booster club officers/activities and provide links to good musical sites on the web. The pages will incorporate original photography and, if possible, musical sound clips.
		• Design site schematic, research and write content and take photographs.
		• Oversee and guide work of Marissa Gordon as she builds these pages.
		12. **DO RESEARCH ON THE WEB TO FIND OUT WHAT THE BEST SCHOOL SITES ARE DOING AND USE THAT INFORMATION TO CONTINUOUSLY IMPROVE THE MOHONASEN SITE.**
		• Also participate in BOCES Communications Service web site planning/brainstorming and problem-solving team.
		DELAYED UNTIL NEXT YEAR...
		1. **CREATE *"MOHONASEN SPORTS"* PAGES**
		2. **CREATE *"MOHONASEN HISTORY"* PAGES**
		3. **ADD JOB POSTINGS PAGE** with link to BOCES web page job openings (list Mohonasen openings there, too??)

Page 4 of 4
Goal #3

EXHIBIT 3.1. Continued

M·O·H·O·N·A·S·E·N 1998-99 Communications Plan · DRAFT

Developed by the Capital Region BOCES Communications Service · 9/98

District Goals	Communication Needs	Communication Projects
CREATE AND MAINTAIN AN ENVIRONMENT THAT IS CONDUCIVE TO LEARNING, SAFE FOR ALL AND DRUG-FREE. • *Implement the Valentine Disipline Model at all grade levels in the middle school...* • *Communicate the presence of a new School Resource (Police) Officer in our schools...* • *Support the work of the Safe Schools 2000 Goal Team...*	Polls show it over and over – school safety is the number one concern of parents around the country. Parents need to know that school officials take their concerns seriously and are capable of maintaining order in our schools. The public expects zero tolerance for bullying, harassment, violence and drug use in our schools. Locally, Mohonasen is doing a lot to address just these kinds of concerns. The onus is on the district to make sure parents and others know just what is being done to ensure school safety and discipline. Better communication on these issues will help ensure compliance with the district's code of student conduct and build public confidence in our schools' ability to maintain a safe and productive school environment.	To help the district reach this goal, the Communications Service will undertake the following projects in 1998-99: 1. **WRITE RELATED STORIES FOR THE DISTRICT NEWSLETTER AND/OR WEB SITE** as appropriate and time allows. Story ideas include: • The new smoking policy that will result in fines for students. • "A-day-in-the-life" story on the new uniformed school resource officer to explain what that person's role is and what impact he or she is having on students. • The expanding Valentine discipline program at the middle school. 2. **WORK WITH LOCAL REPORTERS TO SECURE ACCURATE AND TIMELY COVERAGE** on school initiatives related to safe and drug-free schools. 3. As appropriate, **PUBLICIZE THE RECOMMENDATIONS OF THE SAFE SCHOOLS 2000 GOAL TEAM** which has been reviewing the Safe Schools Committee Report. 4. As appropriate, **PUBLICIZE THE FINDINGS OF THE EFFICIENCY STUDY GRANT ON AT-RISK STUDENTS** and implementation of the subsequent action plan.

EXHIBIT 3.1. Continued

M·O·H·O·N·A·S·E·N 1998-99 Communications Plan · DRAFT

Developed by the Capital Region BOCES Communications Service · 9/98

District Goals	Communication Needs	Communication Projects
Build informed consent for Mohonasen's 1999-00 budget and encourage voting on May 18, 1999. * * * *Develop a budget that addresses educational and operational needs at a tax rate that can be approved by voters.*	Over a period of many months, Mohonasen works with a Budget Review Committee to develop a school budget that is both educationally and fiscally responsible. The district welcomes public comment throughout the budget process. Once the Board of Education adopts a budget (April 5) for residents to vote on (May 18), a great deal of energy goes into building informed consent for the budget proposition through face-to-face communications, district publications and the news media. Residents need to know: • what they will be voting on; and • why it is important to vote. Both print and person-to-person communications focus on the nuts-and-bolts of the budget: what's new in the budget (and why), what's been cut (if anything), what the district is doing to contain costs, what residents get for their school tax dollars, what it will cost, how to get answers to questions about the budget, who the candidates are for the Board of Education, when and where to vote, etc.	To help the district reach this goal, the Communications Service will undertake the following projects in 1998-99 (concentrated in March, April and May): 1. **DEVELOP AND IMPLEMENT A COMPREHENSIVE COMMUNICATIONS PLAN,** modeled on the 1997-98 budget campaign, that reaches large numbers of people in the community through both print and person-to-person communications. Key elements to include: • **CRAFT KEY MESSAGE POINTS** with administration. • **EDIT AND DESIGN POWERPOINT/MULTIMEDIA PRESENTATION** that explains the proposed budget. This will be the centerpiece of presentations in the spring. • **HELP SCHEDULE PRESENTATIONS** to all major constituent groups (internal and external). • **USE DISTRICT WEB SITE** to provide information about the proposed budget. Specifically, put all budget publications on-line as well as the PowerPoint presentation. • **WRITE, PHOTOGRAPH AND PRODUCE A 12-PAGE NEWSLETTER** devoted to the budget vote. This publication will provide a comprehensive overview along with a series of "questions and answers" that address common concerns, misconceptions, etc. that have been picked up on along the way. • **WRITE AND PRODUCE AN 8-1/2 X 14" BUDGET BROCHURE** that provides a brief and compelling overview of the budget and lists board candidates. • **GET-OUT-THE-VOTE** phone calls organized through PTO/Homeroom parents. • **SECURE VOTE NOTICE ON SCHOOL MENUS.** • **CREATE HIGH BRIDGE NEWSLETTER AD.** • **SECURE VOTE SIGNS AT ALL SCHOOL BUILDINGS & 1ST CLASS PRODUCTS.** • **CREATE FULL PAGE INSERT FOR INDIVIDUAL SCHOOL NEWSLETTERS.** • **CREATE REMINDER TO VOTE FLYER** to go home in backpacks, K-8 and to all staff. • **WRITE ASSORTED PRESS RELEASES AND WORK WITH THE PRESS** to ensure accurate and ongoing news coverage on this topic.

EXHIBIT 3.1. Continued

M·O·H·O·N·A·S·E·N 1998-99 Communications Plan · DRAFT

Developed by the Capital Region BOCES Communications Service · 9/98

District Goals	Communication Needs	Communication Projects
ASSIST WITH WRITING AND PRODUCTION OF A K-12 SCHOOL-TO-CAREERS HANDBOOK *Also:* *• Continue to expand the number of school-to-career pathways.*	Mohonasen has earned a reputation as a leader in school-to-careers programming. Administrators frequently speak at state and national conferences and consult with school officials from other districts. Toward this end, the district has been working to compile a handbook on Mohonasen's K-12 school-to-careers system. The purpose of this handbook is to: • document how Mohonasen went about developing its school-to-careers system; • serve as a reference/model for other districts and educational organizations; and • serve as a resource to help district staff (as well as other relevant publics) understand this complex and evolving system. Mohonasen intends to copyright the information and provide it for sale to other schools and organizations.	To help the district reach this goal, the Communications Service will: 1. **WORK COLLABORATIVELY WITH A TEAM OF ADMINISTRATORS** to plan, organize, write/edit and design a comprehensive manual showcasing Mohonasen's evolving and expanding K-12 school-to-careers system. The final product will be modeled on the 1998-99 School-to-Careers calendar and be similar in appearance to the Elementary Language Arts Handbooks.

EXHIBIT 3.1. Continued

M·O·H·O·N·A·S·E·N 1998-99 Communications Plan · DRAFT

Developed by the Capital Region BOCES Communications Service · 9/98

District Goals	Communication Needs	Communication Projects
CLOSE OUT THE $14.9 MILLION CONSTRUCTION PROJECT AND EFFECTIVELY IMPLEMENT THE $20.1 MILLION PROJECT. *DEVELOP A PLAN FOR USE OF THE NEW SWIMMING POOL....*	Mohonasen is in the middle of two major construction projects that, combined, will bring $35 million in new classrooms space, a swimming pool, large group learning center and other assorted renovations and improvements. The district will need to communicate regularly with the public as the construction begins on the new project. Parents, students and staff will want to know how construction will impact instruction and when various pieces of the project are scheduled for completion. The district also wants to keep the broader community informed on the progress of the project since the community will have access to the new pool, large group learning center, etc. Special attention will also need to be paid to communicating the fact that the district IS keeping its promise of not raising school taxes as a result of these construction projects.	To help the district reach this goal, the Communications Service will: 1. **REPORT CONSTRUCTION PROGRESS ON THE DISTRICT WEB SITE** including timelines for completion and a photo gallery of work in progress. 2. **REPORT CONSTRUCTION NEWS IN THE DISTRICT NEWSLETTER** such as the scope of the project, general timelines, photographs, and information on how these projects will impact education in the district. 3. **REPORT ON THE RECOMMENDATIONS OF A COMMITTEE TO STUDY STUDENT AND COMMUNITY USE OF THE NEW SWIMMING POOL** using both the district web site, district newsletter and local media.

EXHIBIT 3.1. Continued

M·O·H·O·N·A·S·E·N 1998-99 Communications Plan · DRAFT

Developed by the Capital Region BOCES Communications Service · 9/98

District Goals	Communication Needs	Communication Projects
INCREASE NEWSPAPER COVERAGE OF BOARD PRESENTATIONS AND EDUCATIONAL INITIATIVES.	Both *The Daily Gazette* and *The Rotterdam Journal* have high circulation rates in Rotterdam. The administration wants to use these newspapers more effectively to help inform the community about new programs and initiatives to improve learning. Many of these new programs and initiatives are spotlighted at board of education meetings throughout the year. Yet public attendance at board meetings is predictably low and reporters are often unable to attend due to conflicts with other school/ town meetings. Therefore the word often does not get out.	To help the district reach this goal, the Communications Service will: 1. **DISCUSS CONCERNS ABOUT SPARSE NEWSPAPER COVERAGE** with reporters at both the *Gazette* and *Journal*. Also work more proactively with the regional education reporter at the *Gazette*. 2. **USE THE WEB TO PUBLICIZE BOARD ACTIONS/PRESENTATIONS** both in advance and after the meetings. 3. **PROVIDE MORE WRITTEN PRESS RELEASES ON BOARD ACTIONS/PRESENTATIONS** to help entice reporters into writing a story on a particular program or initiative. Written press releases will also help direct the reporters to a particular story while providing more background information than is typically found in the board agenda. With both local reporters admittedly strapped for time, the goal is to make it as easy as possible for them to write stories on "the important stuff." 4. **KEEP A RUNNING LIST OF STORY IDEAS** and pitch them to local reporters regularly. Work with the superintendent and building principals to get ideas for these stories. 4. **KEEP A FILE OF NEWSPAPER CLIPPINGS** and include these in quarterly reports.

44

EXHIBIT 3.1. Continued

M·O·H·O·N·A·S·E·N 1998-99 Communications Plan · DRAFT

Developed by the Capital Region BOCES Communications Service · 9/98

OTHER Annual Communication Projects

● **WRITE ANNUAL COMMUNICATIONS PLAN AND QUARTERLY REPORTS.**

● **COORDINATE PRODUCTION OF 12-PAGE TRANSPORTATION ISSUE AND 4-PAGE SCHOOL LUNCH FORM.**

● **2ND-LINE LIAISON WITH BOCES PRINT MANAGEMENT SERVICE.**

● **ASSIST WITH "CRISIS COMMUNICATIONS" AS NEEDED.**

● **OTHER ANTICIPATED PUBLICATIONS WORK**

• Goals 2000 volunteer recruitment flyers updated.

• Goals 2000 pancake breakfast flyer updated

• Create handouts/information packet for opening day for staff on Sept. 2nd.

• Update EPIC Parenting Workshop flyer.

• Homework Night for Parents flyers (2 versions/Grades 6 and 7/8).

• Update 1000 Book Child Project flyer.

• Produce summer enrichment brochure.

• Board of Education Certificates of Achievement as needed.

• Search brochure(s), as needed

● **OTHER ANTICIPATED WORK**

• Supervise the work of technology intern Marissa Gordon.

• Supervise the work of a Mohonasen CEIP intern during the second half of the school year.

EXHIBIT 3.1. Continued

M·O·H·O·N·A·S·E·N 1998-99 Communications Plan · DRAFT

Developed by the Capital Region BOCES Communications Service · 9/98

TENTATIVE PRODUCTION SCHEDULE FOR MAJOR PUBLICATIONS & PROJECTS

1st QUARTER – JULY THRU SEPT.

July/August Newsletter (8-pg.)	Mails @ 7/22
Bus Schedules/Lunch Form (16-pg.)	Mails @ 8/19
Calendar (24-pg.)	Mails @ 8/29
Staff Day Packet	Ready for 9/3
Media Relations/Press Releases	Ongoing

Web site:

- Two web sites merged into one .... Done on 9/10/98
- Develop WEB action plan for "98-99 year & beyond ... Complete by 9/25
- Update FAQs section of site .... September 1998
- Maintain What's News/other key pages .... Ongoing
- Explore database driven site/partnerships .... Ongoing
- Write content/plan schematic for Music Pages .... In progress

2nd QUARTER – OCT. THRU DEC.

October Newsletter (8-pg.)	Mails 10/20
December Newsletter (8-pg.)	Mails @
Career Pathways Brochure	Printed Nov. "99
STAR Brochure	Done @
Prepare overview of literacy initiative for media	Done Oct. '98
Fact Sheet on New Testing/Graduation Requirements by Grade Level (grade 6-12)	Done Dec. '98
Media Relations/Press Releases	Ongoing

Web site:

- Maintain What's News/other key pages .... Ongoing
- Explore database driven site/partnerships .... Ongoing
- Consult @ Guidelines for bldg.-level pgs .... December 98
- Update content for one "Visit our Schools" pages .... December 98
- Write/Develop the Construction Project Page .... 2nd Qtr. +
- Mohonasen Music Pages .... Ongoing
- Improve What Do You Think Page/new cgi script .... Done @
- Redesign Directory Page .... Done @
- Address Miscelaneous Design Needs .... Done @
- Research Best Educational Sites on the Web .... Ongoing
- Respond to/manage web e-mails & feedback .... Ongoing

EXHIBIT 3.1. Continued

M·O·H·O·N·A·S·E·N 1998-99 Communications Plan · DRAFT

Developed by the Capital Region BOCES Communications Service · 9/98

TENTATIVE PRODUCTION SCHEDULE FOR MAJOR PUBLICATIONS & PROJECTS

3rd QUARTER – JAN. THRU MARCH

District Report Card(s):

March 1 Statewide Report Card Data Released to the Public

· Research information and interview all principals .... Jan. '99
· Produce detailed report card of student results .... Feb. '99
· Assist with presentations(?) .... Feb. '99

February Newsletter (8-12-pg.) .... Mails @ 2/28

Update HS Course Guide/Handbook (BOCES project) .... Printed _____
(*Ready for HS Orientation Night for 8th-grade parents on March. 2???)

Begin Budget Communications Planning .... March '99

Begin Goals 2000/Year 2000 Planning .... Jan. '99

Media Relations/Press Releases .... Ongoing

Web site:

· Develop templates for teacher web pages .... Jan. 99?
· Maintain What's News/other key pages .... Ongoing
· Consult on Guidelines for Building-level pages .... Ongoing?
· Update content for two "Visit our Schools" pages ...... 3rd Qtr.
· Register site with Major Internet Search Engines ...... Jan. '99
· Review/monitor bldg-lvel pages as appropriate .... Ongoing
· Respond to/manage web e-mails & feedback .... Ongoing

4th QUARTER – APRIL THRU JUNE

Budget:

· Assist with Powerpoint Presentations on Budget ...... Ready @ 4/6*
· **May Budget Newsletter** (12-pg.) .... Mails @ 5/4
· **2-color Budget Brochure** .... Ready @ 5/4*

Web site:

· Maintain What's News/other key pages .... Ongoing
· Review/monitor bldg-lvel pages as appropriate .... Ongoing
· Update Budget Info. in Fast FAQS .... Early May
· Put Budget Powerpoint Presentations on-line .... Early May
· Update content for last "Visit our Schools" pages ..... 3rd Qtr.
· Respond to/manage web e-mails & feedback .... Ongoing

Begin '99-00 Calendar Production

· Settle on theme (literacy, technology, Goals 2000?) ... May '99
· Outline content for 10 facing pages .... June 99
· Take photos for 10 facing pages .... June 99

Begin July/Aug. Newsletter .... Mails @ 7/24/99

Continue Goals 2000/Year 2000 Planning .... Jan. '99

EXHIBIT 3.1. Continued

M · O · H · O · N · A · S · E · N 1998-99 Communications Plan · DRAFT

Developed by the Capital Region BOCES Communications Service · 9/98

TENTATIVE NEWSLETTER STORY PLAN

STORY PLAN:

- Write a story on how technology is being used as a tool to achieve higher standards.
- Write a story on the Tolcott Mountain grant and the use of web TV in student homes.
- Write a story about what Mohonasen is doing to ensure all students pass Regents exams, such as the Class of 2000 project. Tie in with the new regulations (expected in November) from the Board of Regents and the budget implications of these regulations, if any.
- Spotlight legislative issues in the district newsletter and on the web site as appropriate.
- Story on the new Odyssey of the Mind teams/competition featuring the value of both student and parent involvement in this program.
- Write a story on the new assessments and the new graduation requirements, the phase-in schedule and what it means for kids. Tie in with the story on the school report cards/student testing results and what they show.
- Write a story on new criteria for placement into honors courses to assure participation is available to all students who want to be challenged. (Report expected in January)
- Report construction project progress in the district newsletter including construction timelines, photographs, and information on how these projects will impact education in the district.
- Spotlight students achievement in the annual year-end awards issue.

JULY/AUGUST 1998
8 Pages

- ANNUAL SCHOLARSHIPS AND AWARDS ISSUE
- Feature story on technology's role in achieving higher standards
- New Board of Education president/vice president
- New athletic director and director of pupil personnel
- Take Note items (PTSO Craft Fair, Homeroom Parents, Businesses Support After-Glows, Earth Day Clean up at MS, Coaches Needed for Odyssey of the Mind, Asbestos Report, Oldendorf Named to Alumni Hall of Fame, Messina Way)

OCTOBER 1998
8 Pages

- What's New for the 1998-99 School Year?
  - New teachers (lower class sizes)
  - New textbooks
  - New state tests
  - New building project
- Odyssey of the Mind
- GE Grant/Talcott Mt. Science Center/Web TV
- We're Listening Feedback Form
- Web sites merged – plug address!
- Feature on what Sports Boosters has funded
- "Take Note" items (1000 Book Project, Caresse, Women's volleyball, Pinewood's 40th photo, Garage Sale to Benefit Hockey League, Budget Review Committee forming)

DECEMBER 1998
8 Pages

- University Connections
- STAR program
- (Full page) We're Listening Feedback Form
- Board vacancy/new board appointee????

FEBRUARY 1999
8 Pages

- REPORT CARD SUMMARY STORY
- New assessments and the new graduation requirements, the phase-in schedule and what it means for kids. Tie in with the story on the school report cards/student testing results and what they show.

MARCH 1999
8 Pages

-
-

MAY 1999
12 Pages

- SPECIAL BUDGET ISSUE

48

Creating A Positive Relationship With the Media

You need a relationship with the media.

—Elaine Houston, WNYT, Albany, New York, Reporter and Coanchor

The last thing Whitehall Central School District Superintendent James Watson wanted to face one Monday morning in early December 1998 was the sudden death of a 16-year-old student. His spirits darkened more when the media started calling.

The small community was rocked by the news. Located northeast of Glens Falls, New York, and close to the Vermont border, Whitehall has 1,000 students. One Sunday, the aspiring young basketball star died unexpectedly of a heart attack while working at a neighborhood grocery store. On Monday, television stations and newspaper reporters began calling.

"The way the media has gotten to be has put a lot of school administrators more on guard," said Watson. "But I knew there was a way of handling the situation, and we needed to be in control without disrupting the school day."

According to Watson, the media wanted to interview students and shoot film of the school inside and outside. He held what he considers an "informal" press conference by inviting all the media to the school. They were escorted first to the superintendent's office and then to the gym, where Watson arranged for students and coaches to answer questions about their friend and classmate. "The media got the same message at the same time," explained Watson. "It serves no purpose not to cooperate with them. We try to give them the information they want in a responsible way. Whatever angle they are working on receives a balanced approach."

WNYT Albany, New York, Television News Director S. Paul Conti was impressed by Watson's response to the media. "Rather than dodge it, he put himself and the teachers in the gym and answered questions. We got everything we needed and then left him alone," said Conti. Conti believes that the problem with school districts is they have a constituency to report to and they become afraid of the media, which often lies at the core of an adversarial media-education relationship. "[The districts] invite us when they want us there, then dodge us on the pressing issues. Given the nature of the media, if schools don't want to deal with us on the breaking news stories, why would we cover the other things?" he added. "WNYT's policy is to work with school districts to get the breaking stories, but," Conti admitted, "If you treat us badly, it'll be a cold day in hell before I go back and do a discretionary story."

The bottom line when dealing with the media is the importance of building relationships and being prepared. "You need a relationship with the media," says WNYT reporter and coanchor Elaine Houston. "Without it, you're doing a disservice to the school, the district, and its constituents."

Establishing a rapport with the media will help in assessing the worthiness of discretionary stories and controlling the most sensitive breaking news stories. So, when that reporter calls, DON'T PANIC!

Discretionary or "Feel Good" Stories: When You Call The Media

---

Developing a good relationship with the media is contingent on many things:

1. *How many schools or other districts are in the area?* On any given day, the media compete with themselves. Conti says that, in the greater Albany capital region, he's accountable to about 284 school districts. So, schools need to be good at delivering a message. According to Sonya Gordon, Washoe County (Nevada) School District communications specialist, local television assignment editors in Reno have told her that they receive an average of 70 press releases each day.

2. *Is the information newsworthy?* Most school and district information is not breaking news, but rather informational news.

3. *Is the news happening at a global level?* If a school is doing something unique, one good way to relay that is to look at what's happening globally and then *localize* it.

For Example: A national educational research group releases a study on the value of students mentoring other students. Your school has been doing that for years, but the media may not be aware. Call them.

"Schools need to learn how to pitch an event as part of a bigger trend," said Albany *Times Union* reporter Rick Karlin. "The media is trend-happy." A *Times Union* reporter for 8 years, Karlin has covered education since 1994. "Don't just send me a fax saying, 'We have eight new computers and can you do a story?' What's the larger issue at hand? How can that be tied to a broader news angle?"

Taking the Steps

1. *Introduce yourself and get to know the reporters who cover education.* Invite them to take a tour of the school. It doesn't require a crisis to have a dialogue. Face-to-face communication is still one of the best tools for building sound community relations.

Washoe County (Nevada) School District Director of Communications Steve Mulvenon said that he and Sonya Gordon, the district's communications specialist, meet with television and print editors and reporters twice a year at lunch to discuss issues and their evolving relationships.

When bringing a reporter into a school, prepare a one-page fact sheet that gives a statistical breakdown of the school or district (see examples in Exhibits 4.1 and 4.2). Reporters will often ask, "How many students are in your district? What's the average class size? What are the most recent test scores? What percentage of graduating seniors are continuing with higher education?" Fact sheets help an administrator easily refer to statistics and reduce time spent answering questions.

(Text continues on page 55)

EXHIBIT 4.1. Washoe County School District "Fast Facts" Fact Sheet
SOURCE: Washoe County School District; used by permission.

Washoe County
School District

A Growing
School District
Committed To
Excellence

Mission Statement

The Washoe County School District guarantees each student the opportunity to achieve his or her potential through a superior education in a safe and challenging environment in order to develop responsible and productive citizens for our diverse and rapidly changing community.

Adopted December, 1996

For Additional Information

Call the Communications Office:
(702) 348-0371 • FAX (702) 348-0397
Or write:
Communications Office
Washoe County School District
425 East Ninth Street • Reno, Nevada 89520

Board of Trustees

A seven member School Board of Trustees is elected by the citizens of Washoe County to make school district policy. The board employs a superintendent, three assistant superintendents and one associate superintendent to administer the district and carry out policy decisions. Trustees meet every two weeks and special board meetings are called as needed. The public is encouraged to attend.

Factoids

• *Expansion Management* magazine gave the Washoe County School District a "Blue Ribbon" rating which means student achievement is very high despite per-pupil funding being in the moderate range.

• Seventy-five percent of our per-pupil dollars are spent on instruction, a higher percentage than any other district in the state.

• Seven Washoe County schools have earned "Blue Ribbon" national recognition from the U.S. Department of Education. They are Hug, Reed and Reno High Schools, Swope Middle School and Brown, Smithridge and Stead Elementary Schools.

• Forty-seven percent of our high school students take the ACT College Entrance Exam. Thirty-eight percent take the SAT.

• Total scores on college entrance exams (ACT and SAT) are higher than state and national averages.

• The Washoe County School District has 12 National Merit Scholars for 1995-96.

• CTBS scores for grades 3 through 8 continue to outpace the national norm in reading, mathematics and language arts.

• Sixty-eight school / community partnerships offer unique opportunities to students in almost every Washoe County school.

• The district's school bus fleet of 220 buses logs 3,800,000 miles per year, transporting 14,000 students to and from school daily.

• District cafeterias serve approximately 3,000 breakfasts and 18,000 lunches per day which computes to over 3.3 million meals per year.

4/97-3,500

EXHIBIT 4.1. Continued

World History .... 1 credit
American History .... 1 credit
U.S. Government .... 1 credit
Art/Humanities .... 1 credit
Computer Literacy .... 1/2 credit
Health or JROTC .... 1/2 credit

Honors Program/Advanced Placement

Every high school offers an Honors Program that provides an academically challenging curriculum for college preparation and most high schools offer Advanced Placement courses which provide an opportunity for students to receive both high school and college credit.

Special Services

A complete special education program is offered at Marvin Picollo School as well as through neighborhood schools. Qualifying students needing extra help in reading or math are served by Title I programs. The district also offers English as a Second Language (ESL) and a Native American Education program.

Budget

The general operating budget for the 1996-97 school year is $208,257,750. Seventy-seven percent of this support comes from local sources, 22% from state sources and a small amount from federal and other sources. Local funds from sales and property taxes make up 72% of the total resources. Per pupil expenditure from the general operating budget is approximately $4,209.

Parental and Community Involvement

Parents are encouraged to be involved in their child's education at all grade levels. Parents may assist in classrooms, as well as become involved with parent organizations, high school booster clubs and parent advisory committees. Businesses and community members may be involved in the schools through Partners in Education. For more information call (702) 353-5533.

SAT Scores	Verbal	Math
WCSD	516	506
State of Nevada	508	507
National	505	508

High School Dropout Rates

1988 – 89	7.3%	1992 – 93	6.6%
1989 – 90	6.1%	1993 – 94	8.6%
1990 – 91	7.8%	1994 – 95	8.4%
1991 – 92	8.3%	1995 – 96	8.1%

Pupil/Teacher Ratio 1996-97

Kindergarten	23:1	Grade 5	26:1
Grade 1	16:1	Grade 6	26:1
Grade 2	16:1	Grades 7–8*	24:1
Grade 3	22:1	Grades 9–12*	23:1
Grade 4	25:1	*Varies by course and grade	

Employees 1996-97

Certified	3,164
Administrators	197
Classified	2,374
TOTAL	5,735

About Our Teachers 1996-97

Master's Degree and above	46.1%
10 or more years teaching experience*	34.3%
Teaching within area of license	99.0%

*Within Washoe County

High School Graduation Requirements

To be awarded a standard high school graduation diploma, a student must earn a total of 22-1/2 credits and receive a passing score on the proficiency test in reading, writing and mathematics. Of these 22-1/2 credits, 15 are required and 7-1/2 are electives. The required courses are as follows:

English/Language Arts	4 credits
Mathematics	2 credits
Science	2 credits
Physical Education or JROTC	2 credits

The Washoe County School District includes the Reno/Sparks metropolitan area, Incline Village, Gerlach, Empire and Wadsworth.

Currently, there are 56 elementary schools, 11 middle schools, 10 high schools and an occupational center.

Official Enrollment 1996-97

Elementary Schools	28,977
Middle Schools	7,706
High Schools	12,893
TOTAL	49,671*

*Includes 95 ungraded students

Growth

1970 Enrollment	29,112
1980 Enrollment	31,508
1990 Enrollment	38,466
2000 Projection	59,154

Ethnic Breakdown 1996-97

American Indian/Alaskan Native	2.59%
Asian/Pacific Islander	4.81%
Black, not Hispanic	3.54%
Hispanic	16.41%
Total Minorities	27.35%
White, not Hispanic	72.65%

Student Achievement for 1995-96

CTBS Scores (Total Battery) *These scores are percentiles with 50 being the national average.*

Grade 3	57	Grade 6	58
Grade 4	52	Grade 7	59
Grade 5	59	Grade 8	57

ACT Scores (Composite) *Composite scores include English, math, reading and science.*

WCSD	21.6
State of Nevada	21.2
National	20.9

Regal Cinema Project Fact Sheet
May 11, 1999

Description:

The Reno Redevelopment Agency, DDR-OliverMcMillan, and Regal Cinemas have joined forces to bring an exciting new theater project to downtown Reno. Regal Cinemas will establish a 2,200 seat state-of-the-art 12 screen multiplex theater along the north bank of the Truckee River between Sierra and West Streets. The structure is designed to blend with the historic nature of Reno's riverfront developments. This 50,000 square foot project is a major portion of the five block downtown redevelopment effort, and will enjoy easy access to the City's 650-space parking garage just across First Street. Combined with restaurants, recreational opportunities, living space and shopping, the Regal Cinemas theater will help revitalize downtown Reno, bringing life back to the banks of the Truckee River.

Steel Framework Work To Begin:

Ledcor Industries, Incorporated will begin installing the steel framework this week. This will give Reno residents a feel for the size and shape of the building as it rises from the banks of the Truckee River. The site work has been completed and the foundation poured. Now the actual construction of the building begins, and we will be able to witness the progress as the building begins to take shape.

EXHIBIT 4.2. Continued

Finances:

▸ The Redevelopment Agency sold land to OliverMcMillan Group for $1.00.

▸ OliverMcMillan will lease the space to Regal Theaters.

▸ Regal Cinemas will make a lease payment of 8 percent of their gross income. OliverMcMillan will receive $10,000 per year management fee. The Redevelopment Agency will receive the next $150,000 per year.

▸ Over this amount, the Redevelopment Agency receives 60 percent, OliverMcMillan receives 40 percent.

▸ After five years OliverMcMillan will refinance the site and the Redevelopment Agency will receive a minimum of $3 million.

▸ Lease payments will then be paid 60 percent to the Redevelopment Agency, 40 percent to OliverMcMillan.

▸ $10.5 million construction:

> $1.5 million site improvements by Reno Redevelopment Agency
> $6.5 million loan by Reno Redevelopment Agency
> $2.5 million funded by Regal Cinemas

Regal Cinemas, Inc:

▸ Regal Cinemas, Inc. is the largest and one of the fastest growing motion picture exhibitors in the world. The company operates one of the most profitable theater circuits in the industry.

▸ Regal Cinemas was founded by Chairman, CEO and President Michael Campbell in 1989. Campbell started out in grocery retailing, but decided to put his business knowledge to work in the cinema by purchasing a broken down local movie theater. Campbell repaired it and began a successful chain of small market movie theaters, Premiere Cinemas, which he sold to begin a much larger movie venture, Regal Cinemas, Inc.

▸ Regal's management instituted very tight financial controls, managed the theaters as retail establishments and fully developed the concept of multi-screen motion picture theaters.

▸ Regal Cinemas' focus has been mid-size metropolitan markets and suburban areas primarily in the eastern U.S. The theaters are predominantly large multiplexes.

• In 1995 Regal Cinemas was listed in Forbes Magazine as one of the 200 best small companies. In 1998 Regal Cinemas combined with ACT III. Together they own about 3,200 screens at approximately 400 theaters in 29 states. Regal Cinemas also operates FunScape centers, which house movie theaters, miniature golf courses, and virtual reality games.

If you don't have a public information officer, appoint a lead or contact person to serve as a liaison to the media. In many smaller schools or school districts, that responsibility will fall to the principal. That person then becomes a point of reference for all future discussions between the school/district and the media.

2. *Send the media copies of your newsletter or other appropriate materials.* Plenty of things wouldn't require a "hard news" story but might get their attention for another story later. Brochures detailing programs and services, as well as budget charts and test scores, can be used as reference tools. *Remember* that a school district is accountable to its shareholders—taxpayers and parents—and that they are entitled to this information.

3. *Develop a media list.* Include assignment editors and education reporters' names, addresses, and telephone and fax numbers, as well as e-mail addresses. Once you've established rapport with some reporters, learn their deadlines and contact them accordingly.

Television stations, radio stations, and newspaper publishers operate under different deadlines. "We usually have a 5:30 or 6:00 p.m. deadline for stories," said Karlin. If they are rushed or on deadline, they are less likely to hear your pitch. Calling a television newsroom 1 hour before the evening news broadcast will most likely end in frustration or unreturned phone calls. Often resembling bedlam, a newsroom is simply too busy preparing for that broadcast.

4. *Mail, fax, or e-mail press releases, media advisories, or details about photo opportunities on important events.* Do not waste the media's time with frivolous requests. Sending too much information can backfire. Ask yourself, "Is this something I'd be interested in reading about or watching?" According to Schenectady, New York, *Daily Gazette* reporter Brian Nearing, school administrators should try to think in terms of "the best, the biggest, the first," because it gets noticed. "I'd be interested in a story where a math teacher has an abacus collection and uses them as part of the classroom," said Nearing. "That's unusual. But students giving presents at Christmas is normal. Everyone is doing it."

"There's only so many times you can go to the media with the same story," said Paula Sulinski, founder and president of Third Street Marketing and Media Services in Detroit, Michigan. With 25 years of broadcasting experience, Sulinski also serves as a public relations consultant to school districts. "Schools need to learn how to frame a story and play all aspects of it. Give the media compelling reasons to cover it."

WNYT Television News Director S. Paul Conti agreed. "Have realistic expectations. When the first school donated food and supplies to Kosovo refugees, we were there. It was a big story. We may not, however, cover the fourth or fifth school to do the same thing."

Make the press release or advisory timely, short, and informational—Who, What, Where, When, and How—with a contact person's name and telephone number prominently displayed. Try to keep a release to a single page with only the most pertinent information. A reporter will write her or his own story. Include additional information if necessary.

For Example: A school is discussing the construction of a new wing and is having an open house. Include a copy of the architectural renderings.

A bad press release can do more damage then not sending one at all. Exhibit 4.3 is an example of what *not* to do. The most glaring problem with the release is references, or lack thereof. Who sent it? Where did it originate? Who's the contact person if the media have questions? What is the date of the release? Where does the release end? Where is Metropolitan Elementary School located? In what city/town is the school or hospital located? What's the street address? What time does the performance start? Does the performance have anything to do with a larger story (e.g., if the students are performing as the culmination of a 6-week

EXHIBIT 4.3. Example of a Bad Press Release

—PRESS RELEASE—

Metropolitan Elementary School 6th Graders
Will Sing at Veterans Hospital

Students in Mr. Jones' sixth-grade class will be singing songs to patients at the Veterans Hospital on Saturday, July 3. The children have been working very hard to find and prepare songs that have a military theme and honor our beloved veterans. It's because of them we live in a free and democratic country.

Our students rehearse for 2 hours each day and some of them wrote their own songs for the veterans. They will be dressed in red, white, and blue costumes that their parents made for them. The students will be there at the same time that Senator Howard will be visiting the hospital. The kids will have lots of fun and we think the patients will really enjoy the performance. We think the television stations and newspapers should come too!

---

arts-in-education history assignment as part of a new state curriculum mandate)? Does the school have a partnership with the hospital, and have the two organizations been working on projects? Why must the reader go to the second paragraph to see that the performance is part of Senator Howard's visit? The release includes editorial comments such as "It's because of them we live in a free and democratic society" and "The kids will have lots of fun and we think the patients will really enjoy the performance. We think the television stations and newspapers should come too!" The comments are irrelevant to getting the media there. The media want facts. If you are presenting an emotional appeal, write a comment as a quote and attribute it to someone (e.g., the release could include a quote from one of the patients, such as, "It's nice to know in this day and age our efforts were not lost on this generation").

If a school event does not merit a story but has strong emotional or visual appeal, send a photo opportunity or media advisory release (see examples in Exhibits 4.4 and 4.5). A photo "op" is similar to a press release but clearly outlines the visual appeal. There's no need to go into great detail on the event; it's self-evident.

For Example: A Siberian tiger cub from Safari County Zoo is visiting third-grade students, who will give the cub a name. It's not an in-depth story but has great visual appeal.

Press releases are designed to get the media's attention. When reporters are on tight deadlines, they may quote directly from the release, so be sure all information is accurate. To make the release more interesting, use quotes from students or teachers to help illustrate a point.

When writing a press release, adhere to a newspaper-style format. Start the release with the most important information first. Use letterhead or another easily identifiable logo that indicates the source of the release. Be sure that all names are spelled correctly. Invariably, the general content of the information could be correct, but if someone sees her or his name spelled incorrectly, that person will never let you forget it. Be sure that any math or numbers are correct as well. Clearly mark that it's a *Press Release, News Release, Media Advisory,* or *Photo Opportunity* at the top of the page, with a brief headline beneath it (see Exhibit 4.6). If it is time sensitive, add URGENT (only for breaking news stories) or FOR IMMEDIATE RELEASE. Be sure to include the date of the release and a contact person, telephone number, and address (see Exhibits 4.6, 4.7,

EXHIBIT 4.4. Washoe County School District News Release, "Hey Bard-Tender!"
SOURCE: Washoe County School District; used by permission.

NEWS RELEASE

||||||||||||||||||||||||||||||||||||||||||||||||||||||||||||||||||||||||||||||||||||||||||||||||||||||||||||||||||||||||

Washoe County School District
425 East Ninth Street • Reno, NV 89520
Date: May 7, 1999   **Communications/Information Office**
                                       (702) 348-0371 • (FAX) 348-0397

Contact: Steve Mulvenon/Sonya T. Gordon

'HEY, BARD-TENDER!'
TALENT ACADEMY STUDENTS PERFORM SHAKESPEARE

RENO-SPARKS -- "Zany Scenes from Shakespeare," a collection of
scenes from "MacBeth" to "A Midsummer Night's Dream," will be
presented by the district's Talent Academy in a one-hour production at
7 p.m. Friday and Saturday, May 14 and 15. It will be held at the Eardley
Auditorium in the Red Mountain Building at TMCC.

The production is the culmination of a year's worth of the Talent Academy's
acting lessons, memorizations and practice. It features 60 students from
the Academy in fourth, fifth and sixth grades. These students have been
identified for their ability and potential in conducting outstanding arts
performances.

Tickets are $6 for adults and $3 for children 12 and younger. **For more**
information or to reserve a seat, call 829-9024.

-30-

EXHIBIT 4.5. City of Reno Media Advisory on Regal Cinema Project
SOURCE: City of Reno, Nevada; used by permission.

Media Advisory
City of Reno
Christopher Good
Public Communication Coordinator
Voice 775.326.6309
Fax 775.321.8324
May 11, 1999

MEDIA OPPORTUNITY
REGAL CINEMA PROJECT FINALLY '*OFF THE GROUND*'
The custom-built steel frames have been delivered to the job site. The humongous
construction crane is lying in wait. By the end of this week Renoites will see the Regal Cinemas
multiplex project rise from the banks of the Truckee River, near the corner of First and Sierra
Streets.

Work crews will begin installing the steel frame for the 12-screen multiplex this week,
giving us all a sense for the building's size and shape. The media are invited to photograph the
progress, with work beginning Wednesday, May 12. Friday, May 14 is the suggested day for
good photographs. The recommended place to get nice shots is the Parking Gallery, just across
First Street from the construction site.

A fact sheet follows this page.

-30-

and 4.8). If a press release is more than one page, indicate "more" at the bottom of the first page (see Exhibit 4.8). At the end of the release, write #, -30-, or -End-; the media will then recognize there is nothing further (see Exhibits 4.6 and 4.7)

5. *Follow up with a telephone call—"By the way, did you receive my press release?"* Following up with the reporter is important because press releases can easily get lost in the "black hole" of a newsroom, and a call serves as a reminder.

6. *Create a weekly "tip sheet" for slow news days.* Tip sheets should include a week's worth of short, attention-getting blurbs on events that aren't particularly newsworthy but that can be fun and informational "filler" (see Exhibit 4.8).

7. *Learn to "niche" or use news "pegs."* Not everything your school does will excite everyone. Learning how to niche activities can bring huge dividends.

For Example: One Albany High School junior took top honors in a cooking contest. Students win awards all the time. But this story got more attention once it was pitched to one of the food editors in the "Life and Leisure" section of the local newspaper, which ran the story, including his recipes on the front page of the "Lifestyles" section. This approach holds true for business reporters (school-to-work stories), technology reporters (computers in the classroom stories), and health reporters (students donate money to AIDS patients stories).

8. *Avoid using educational jargon.* Simply put, don't use it. Enough said.

9. *Understand the differences in media logistics.* Television, radio, and print media operate differently, and their readiness and ability to cover a story often have to do with logistics. Print reporters often have more flexibility on discretionary stories; they can delve, investigate, and spend more time on researching a topic. Television, in contrast, is all *visual*.

"Make teachers and students available to us," said KTVN-TV Channel 2 Reno News Director Nancy Cope. "Without them, we have a story of talking management heads. Boring! Another problem is that school stories are often issue-related, and that means boring video. We're a visual medium. We need good pictures to keep viewers interested."

Radio can be a powerful medium. Consider talking with the local talk-radio personality to generate news. Public and commercial radio also have subtle differences. "We have more time available to us on public radio," said KUNR Reno, Nevada, Station Manager David Gordon. "Commercial radio stations are primarily concerned with paid messages first and foremost. In public broadcasting, we're not worried about commercials. We have the luxury of time." Gordon added that commercial radio deals with news in more of a "what's happened" mode. "That's why you'll see radio and television stations with helicopters covering high-speed chases. They are reporting *as* it's happening, not *why* it's happening. That's where we step in."

Accessing public radio to get your school's message across is contingent on several things: (a) the number of other public radio stations in the area and (b) their formats. Most radio stations have an outlet for public service announcements, although public stations broadcast more because of Federal Communications Commission (FCC) requirements. If a commercial station has an all-news format, however, the likelihood of getting your message out is greater.

"By and large, school districts will benefit from working with public radio stations because they can discuss issues and concerns without breaking to go to a commercial," said Gordon. "Air time is difficult to fill

(Text continues on page 63)

EXHIBIT 4.6. Washoe County School District News Release, "Drop-Out Rate Improves"
SOURCE: Washoe County School District; used by permission.

NEWS RELEASE

||||||||||||||||||||||||||||||||||||||||||||||||||||||||||||||||||||||||||||||||||||||||||||||||||||||||||||||

Washoe County School District
425 East Ninth Street • Reno, NV 89520
Communications/Information Office
(702) 348-0371 • (FAX) 348-0397

Date: January 26, 1999

Contact: Steve Mulvenon/Sonya T. Gordon

DROP-OUT RATE IMPROVES BY
MORE THAN 1 PERCENT IN WASHOE COUNTY SCHOOLS

RENO-SPARKS -- What a difference a year makes. The drop-out rate across the Washoe County School District in 1997-1998 improved by more than one percentage point over the 1996-1997 school year: from 8.5 percent to 7.3 percent.

According to the school district's Planning, Research & Evaluation Department, **all but two of the 10 high schools had lower drop-out rates for the 1997-1998 school year over the previous year.**

After a follow-up investigation was conducted at two high schools that had substantially lower rates, it was determined the improvement was due to: much stronger student support through calls to the home, accelerated student counseling of potential drop outs and more accurate follow-up of students who had entered correctional facilities or the Washoe Adult Program (who should not be counted as drop outs).

The schools with the lowest drop-out rates were: the Truckee Meadows Community College High School at 0 percent, Incline High School at 1.4 percent, Galena High School at 1.8 percent and Gerlach High School at 2.1 percent. **The most decrease in drop-out rates** for 1996-1997 vs. 1997-1998 occurred at Gerlach High School (from 14.3 percent to 2.1 percent) and Wooster High School (from 10.9 percent to 6.5 percent).

-30-

Washoe County School District
Communications/Information Office
425 East Ninth Street • Reno, NV 89520

Date: May 7, 1999

Phone (702) 348-0371
Fax (702) 348-0397

Contact: Steve Mulvenon or Sonya T. Gordon
NOTE TO EDITORS: This is the second A, B, C's briefs press release sent out today.

WASHOE COUNTY SCHOOL DISTRICT'S A, B, C's
Three Briefs of Note About WCSD Staff, Teachers and Students

A. Cow Pie Bingo

Moo-ove it to Reed High School this weekend to play Cow Pie Bingo, a fund-raiser to benefit the school's National Junior ROTC program. You'll be hefting a hefty "heifer" into the air and throwing it onto a makeshift bingo card to determine the winning squares for prizes and **a chance to win $500.** That's big moo-la! The school parking lot will be transformed into one large bingo card. This game is not for cow-ards!

To play this udder-ly ridiculous game, just show up at Reed High School's parking lot (1350 Baring Blvd. in Sparks) 10 a.m.-noon Saturday, May 8. Admission is free. For more information, call Delores Martinez at 329-6626.

B. Get Your Just Desserts!

Verdi Elementary School will be holding its Open House / Dessert Night / Science Festival 6:30-8:30 p.m. Tuesday, May 11. This "Under the Sea" night will include cookies and cakes for those with a sweet tooth, plus Oceans Week displays of projects and collections. **For more information, call 345-8100.**

C. All-llll Aboard For Families On Board!

Parents and children have a chance to work together with teachers as partners in the educational process thanks to Families on Board. This free, hands-on program was developed by the Washoe County School District and Family Counseling Services. Families on Board provides strategies for parents to increase their child's success in school. Parents will learn ways to help with homework and partner with their child's teacher. The program also includes B.A.G.S., a separate workshop emphasizing that Books Are Good Stuff to children ages 3 to 11.

Agnes Risley Elementary will be offering the 90-minute workshops beginning next week -- 6-7:30 p.m. Monday, May 10, and Tuesday, May 11. This is no cost to attend. Participants will be able to enter a drawing for great raffle prizes given away on Tuesday night. All parents attending both nights will receive a new book for their child courtesy of KNPB-Channel 5. **To register, call Norma at Risley ES, 353-5760 or, for more information, call Sherry Cushman at 348-0379.**

-30-

EXHIBIT 4.8. Reno's *City Tips*, May 22, 1998
SOURCE: City of Reno, Nevada; used by permission.

P.O. Box 1900
Reno, Nevada, 89505

News and Information
City of Reno
Christopher Good
Public Communication Coordinator
702-326-6309
Fax: 702-334-2097
May 22, 1998

City Tips

Every Friday we send a list of story ideas that can be useful in developing news reports. Please call the Community Relations Division or contacts provided for more information or visual opportunities.

For This I Get a Meal? There are over 300 volunteers who donate their time, brains and sweat to the ideal of self-government in Reno by working on boards and commissions. Their real reward is living in a community they have improved, but as a gesture of appreciation the City will treat them to dinner at the National Automobile Museum on Thursday, May 28. Doors open at 5:45 p.m., dinner will be served, then the awards ceremony starts at 8:00 p.m. This event will make a great story: a whole roomful of people who stopped complaining and got busy working to make Reno a better place to live.

Here Comes the Judge: Judge Jay Dilworth, Reno Municipal Court Judge for Department One, was selected by the National Center for State Courts to participate in a conference in Orlando, Florida. The participants provided suggestions to improve the Center's Trial Court Performance Standards, which have been adopted by trial courts nationwide. The participants shared their own courts' experiences in designing and implementing innovative court programs. This is an invitation-only conference and we are very proud that Judge Dilworth was selected to represent the City of Reno in this very important function. He should return from Florida on Tuesday, May 26. You can reach his office at 334-2296

Bridge to the 21st Century: OK, it didn't take *that* long. The Center Street Bridge should open for holiday weekend traffic on Friday afternoon. To celebrate, the City Council invites the media to join the party on the bridge at 7:00 p.m. Wednesday, May 27. There will be entertainment, fun and tremendous visual opportunities. We'll see you at the bridge!

Reno's Efficiency Highlighted: Public Works Magazine, a national publication serving engineers, contractors and public works professionals, highlights the City of Reno's infrastructure maintenance system this month. The article describes the City's new system to manage maintenance work on streets, sewers and other infrastructure systems. In the first year we saved over $625,000 by working more efficiently. This makes more money available for street rehabilitation and other work that is sorely needed in Reno. For more information, call Steve Varela, director of Public Works, at 334-2215.

-more-

EXHIBIT 4.8. Continued

City Tips - May 22, 1998
Page 2

To Find the Next Diego Rivera: The Reno Redevelopment Agency is working to get locally-produced art up on the exterior of the Riverside Hotel. Murals will go up in early June on 45 windows facing Virginia Street, lending a creative and colorful tone to the historic building which will be transformed into living/working space for artists. The agency is working with Philip Coleman, professional muralist and teacher at Hug High School. Two of his classes will paint pieces for part of this project as their final exam.. For more information call Chris Good at 326-6309.

Make This Weekend Memorable For the Right Reasons: Last year on Memorial Day Weekend, there were 42 vehicle crashes reported in Reno, 12 DUI arrests, and 359 citations issued. This year the Reno Police Department will be out in force again. They will pay special attention to high-accident locations and those streets where residents have complained about speeders. Also, the Police Department can provide free baby car seats to those people stopped who cannot afford to buy one. This is thanks to a generous donation from Bob and Callie Elam, owners of the Midas Muffler Company of Reno. Please help us help others by publicizing the fact that the Police will be out there checking traffic. Deterrence and education will help reduce the number of accidents on this busy weekend.

A Well-Lit, but Costly False Alarm: At the Reno City Council meeting at noon on Tuesday, May 26, the Council will consider a proposal to upgrade the street lights in the downtown area. They will also discuss the possibility of establishing a $31.00 charge for false alarms to which the Reno Police Department responds, and they are scheduled to vote on the annual budget for the City of Reno.

-30-

every day. You'll stand a much better chance at getting on a station that has a 3-hour hole to fill 5 days a week, rather than a 30-second news sound bite." One disadvantage to radio is that it does not use pictures. "There may be lots of things that lend themselves to a good photo op," said Gordon, "but not radio. One advantage we do have is that there's a lot of uninterrupted time, which can outweigh the disadvantages of video."

Generally, radio reporters do not need to be on-site to do a report. They can call and record a conversation without setting foot on school property. Remember, however, that they are audiotaping the conversation even when you think they aren't. Make sure that what you say is accurate.

10. *Look for opportunities.* The media themselves are often an excellent resource for opportunities. Albany's NBC affiliate WNYT produces weekly *Education Spotlight* segments with education reporter and coanchor Elaine Houston. Focusing on educational issues, the segments are generally 2 minutes in length and run twice a week. Stories vary, but generally, Houston said, she looks for "the unusual." "I'm not looking for information on standardized test scores or the run-of-the-mill stories," she explained. "Too often, teachers or administrators don't call me, and there's a lot of great stories out there. I try to make an effort to reach out to schools, but they need to contact us as well."

Houston cited one example of an *Education Spotlight* story involving a middle school bike club. "I did one story on the Lisha Kill Middle School in the South Colonie School District because they started a bike club. The school's science teacher, James Brown, contacted me and relayed the story of how he and his son paid a visit to a local landfill. While there, his son, Dylan, noticed usable, discarded bikes that had been thrown away."

When asked about the bikes, an attendant at the landfill stated that an average of three to five good bikes was discarded weekly. That ignited Brown's imagination, and shortly thereafter he spoke with the school's D.A.R.E. Officer Brian Casey about the bikes. Casey said that the Colonie (New York) Police Department also discarded at the Colonie dump any stolen or abandoned bikes that had not been claimed.

Together, Brown and Casey came up with the idea to write a grant to make use of the discarded bikes. The idea was to have students repair discarded bikes and then donate them to needy families in the area. At the same time, students would learn about recycling, as well as about categorizing and measuring with the metric system. Eventually, they netted a $10,000 Toyota Tapestry Grant, which helped them underwrite the cost of tools and a 42-ft trailer to store the bikes on property. As the club gained in popularity, the number of bikes donated soared. "At one time, we had 45 active students and 300 bikes in storage," said Brown, "with 20 to 30 students waiting to participate!"

While working as the public information specialist for the City School District of Albany, I had an opportunity to write and coproduce an educational news magazine show called Capital Education's *Spirit of Discovery* on Public Broadcasting Station's WMHT-TV 17. Based in Schenectady, New York, WMHT cosponsored the show by offsetting production costs.

The show ran in two formats: (a) a stand-alone 15-minute piece and (b) a trimmed 5-minute version on WMHT's regional show *Upstate Edition.* The station had a potential audience reach of 500,000 households.

Said former WMHT Educational Services Coordinator Eileen Nash in a *Capital Education* newsletter, "We're interested in coproducing *Spirit of Discovery* because education is central to our mission, and we have increased our commitment to local programming."

One of the biggest draws was content. For three seasons, the show focused on such issues as school finances, arts-in-education, school violence, new teaching methods, and parental involvement. Two community members volunteered their time to host the show, and WMHT provided a director, videographer, and off- and on-line editing.

"*Spirit of Discovery* had a broad appeal to parents, students, teachers, and taxpayers," said former WMHT Associate Producer and Director Tamara Robison. "The show kept people informed. It was a fun project and never boring. Although the show was about the City School District of Albany, it had a greater community outreach. We got requests for copies of the show to be used in classrooms."

Now a senior producer with WOSU Public Television, in Columbus, Ohio, Robison said that the only difficulties were in production. "With only 1 day or two half-days to shoot, it was tough to work around a school schedule. Plus, with some of those old buildings, we couldn't find adequate electrical outlets," she said with a laugh.

Local public educational and government access stations can also deliver a school's message. In Reno, Sierra Nevada Community Access Television (SNCAT) has a variety of educational programs, as well as instruction. "We reach 75,000 homes," said Executive Director Chris Jensen. "It behooves a school district to use a station like SNCAT as a resource, especially since we have expanded air time and there's no charge for it."

Through local cable access agreements, SNCAT offers time slots for educational programs and classes for educators and students to learn television production. "It's interactive," Jensen said. "We work with the school district's Opportunity School and Glenn Hare Occupational Center. They can produce their own shows that highlight school programs, events, teachers, and students. It's a way to emphasize not only what's going on but to give visibility to all the positive things that the schools and district are doing. The students become the creators of the school's message. I'd like to see more of that here, and that's part of our goal at SNCAT."

To find the location of public educational and government access stations nearest to you, contact the Alliance for Community Media. The group has a listing of regions and chapters and is accessible through their Web site at *http://www.alliancem.org*, or 666 11th Street, NW, Suite 806, Washington, DC 20001.

11. *Write opinion editorial pieces in the local newspaper.* One good way to get your message out to the community is through the opinion-editorial (op-ed) section of a newspaper. School administrators cannot expect the media to carry the district's message. "I'm not on the school's payroll," says reporter Rick Karlin. "My job is to be objective, not to get the district's viewpoint across."

Writing an opinion-editorial can directly and passionately deliver a message. "Op-eds are an effective, legitimate way to get a point across," said Karlin.

12. *Write thank-you notes to reporters when they have done a job well, and send a copy of it to their editor at the newspaper or to their news director at the radio or television station.* As in any other business, thank yous can go a long way. More often than not, reporters are criticized for what they did not write or cover, and they need to know when they've done a good job.

13. *Share resources with the local university or college in the area that is doing public relations for their educational teaching and other services.*

14. *Talk with television assignment editors or reporters about appearing on morning or weekend talk/call-in shows.* Many have weekend public awareness shows that are well suited to issue-driven material.

15. *If the media are not available for an event, offer them written or recorded video- or audiotapes for possible use at a later time.*

Hard or Breaking News: When the Media Call You

Never was the axiom "Honesty is the best policy" more true than when dealing with the media. Being forthright and direct is one of the best ways to build credibility and accountability with the public and the media. This concept is the cornerstone of Bleiker philosophy.

"I respond well to directness," said *Gazette* reporter Brian Nearing. "If I ask a question, I expect an answer. If you don't know the answer, say so. Don't just start talking a lot and not saying anything. It wastes my time and insults my intelligence."

Take the Steps

1. *Appoint a lead person or liaison to handle media inquiries so that reporters have an established contact.* Even if that person may not be the most appropriate to handle a particular question, she or he can coordinate to get the best possible resource. Find out who the reporters are, what agency they are with, and what they are asking. Many education reporters will regularly call with ideas for stories that involve some research, and the answer may not be readily available.

2. *Return media calls promptly.* Reporters work on deadlines. "Some superintendents I know never return phone calls from reporters," said Whitehall Central School District Superintendent James Watson. "Then they complain later that the media never covers anything they do. It's important to work with them, and you can do it with integrity."

Albany Times Union reporter Rick Karlin said that if he's working on a story that needs to be written by a 6 p.m. deadline and he called the school/district that morning, it does little good to call the next day. "Stonewalling does nothing for a district and, in fact, draws more attention to a story," said Karlin. In addition, if a district doesn't respond, the press can say the district didn't return phone calls or had no comment, thereby setting up the school for public scrutiny. The perception is, "Well, if they can't comment, what are they hiding?"

3. *If you don't know the answer to a question or it involves someone with more expertise, then tell the reporter you don't know the answer but will connect him or her with the appropriate person.*

For Example: A reporter calls because a study was just released on whole language teaching. The question is whether elementary education in your district uses whole language teaching and why or why not. As liaison, your background may not be in elementary education, so you would refer the reporter to the elementary education director or supervisor, who is more knowledgeable in that area. Then, take the steps necessary to connect the two. It may involve calling the elementary education teacher first and relaying what the reporter is requesting and then asking the director to return the reporter's call.

4. *Get the facts straight.* If you can't be the first source of information (e.g., when a reporter or assignment editor calls you after picking up a report from a police scanner), then be the best source. If you know the answer to the question, answer it honestly and openly, but be sure it's accurate. If you are unsure of your facts, tell the reporter you need to verify information first and will call back immediately with the answer.

DO NOT SAY, "NO COMMENT"! That's like waving a red flag and saying to the media, "We know something and you don't." Even trying to obscure the facts could come back to haunt an administrator because it damages the school's/district's credibility with the public and the media.

There will be times when you can't answer a question, particularly those involving personnel issues, litigation, or child custody cases. Given those situations, it is safe to explain the condition to a reporter, and if the reporter is one you've built a solid relationship with, she or he will understand—as long you make it clear that you cannot release information because of extenuating circumstances.

5. *Determine the best course of action in dealing with a reporter.* Depending on the call, you will need to size up the situation. Is the incident an isolated case that can be handled through meeting with the reporter or over the telephone? Does the incident have a broader impact, such as a fire, bomb threat, or gas leak at a school building? In those cases, would a press conference be necessary, or would simply issuing a district statement to the media be enough? Have a fact sheet available that outlines the incident.

6. *Be prepared for the question behind the question.* "School administrators should be ready to handle the breadth of questioning," said *Gazette* reporter Brian Nearing. "We'll ask questions that are beyond the incident, and a good spokesperson should have background information for the larger picture." According to Nearing, reporters look to the liaison or public information person to help navigate through the layers of bureaucracy.

When a reporter calls on a tough situation, first think through all the potential questions and have solid answers prepared. Then try practicing the interview with someone in your office.

For Example: A high school junior physically attacks another student at lunch while shouting anti-Semitic names. School police remove the disruptive student. A television station picks up the report from a police scanner. You agree to talk with the reporter about the incident. Possible questions to consider *before* the reporter arrives and potential answers:

Reporter: Has this type of incident happened at your school before?

Administrator: No. Our school has a code of conduct, and whether it's physical, emotional, or mental, abuse is not tolerated.

Reporter: What are the consequences for this type of action?

Administrator: According to our school board policy on disciplinary measures for abuse, assault, or possession of a firearm by a student, the student is subject to a minimum of a 1-year suspension. (At this point, the administrator should have a copy of the policy to give to the reporter.)

Reporter: Does this student have a past history of anti-Semitic behavior?

Administrator: Not in school, and our counselors and teachers are required to report any such conduct to the principal. Then, a parent conference is called.

Reporter: What percentage of students attending your school are Jewish?

Administrator: We don't have statistics on our students' religious beliefs.

Reporter: Now that the student has been arrested, what will the school do?

Administrator: Our first priority is to restore order to the school community. We have a crisis management team that consists of teachers and school psychologists. That team will work with students in the school who have been affected by this incident. The disruptive student will have a psychological evaluation before returning to school. We will also notify all parents with a letter that will go home with students today. Under no circumstances will this behavior be tolerated, and the school will take whatever steps are necessary to ensure that it doesn't happen again.

7. *Understand opponents who may be quick to contact the media when something negative arises.* As with any organization, not everyone will like what you do. Administrators can temper that by anticipating negative reaction and communicating with the public and the media. Again, The Bleiker Lifepreserver states that your organization should be "the first with the bad news." If you can't be the first, then be the best source of news.

In 1998, the City School District of Albany (New York) decided to reschedule advanced placement math honors classes at the high school and to combine 9th- and 10th-grade heterogeneous students. According to District Superintendent Lonnie Palmer, "We had seen warning signs when the high school parents began asking questions and assumed that we were eliminating the classes. We didn't react fast enough, and later we saw the story on the front page."

According to *Times Union* reporter Rick Karlin, who covered the story, a parent had called the paper with a tip. "I don't think opponents skew the story if they strike first, if the reporting is thorough, and the reporter gets the other side," said Karlin. "But there is a difference between a skewed story and one that an administration doesn't want to get out. It's a subtle but important difference." Karlin added, "It probably does make sense for an administration to come out with the bad news first. The problem is, what's their definition of bad news? For instance, the honors classes in math are essentially accelerated classes—or ninth graders taking 10th-grade math. By eliminating one of the offerings, I'll concede that the administration might have honestly thought it wasn't that big of a deal, and they may have been blindsided in that regard."

"With a second chance, we would have invited the two local reporters and briefed them on the proposed changes and their purpose," Palmer added. "The purpose was to consolidate classes where the curriculum was the same to improve class balances and to make certain honors and AP (Advanced Placement) classes had a different and more challenging curriculum."

8. *Develop key message points.* Prior to responding to an in-depth question, develop key message points that can be easily referenced (see Exhibit 4.9). Message points should be short and emphasize what you want to see covered. They stress the school's/district's viewpoint and consider what's important for the shareholders (taxpayers and parents) to hear. Make sure all administrators, staff, and teachers are giving the same message to the press.

9. *Control the interview.* Dialogue with the media can be tricky at times. Some things to watch for:

A. If a reporter asks you to respond to a comment made by another individual that you weren't present to hear, it's best to not comment at all.

For Example: A reporter calls you and says that the president of the middle school PTA thinks the district isn't doing enough to help build middle school students' test scores. The reporter asks you to respond to the comment. The comment may or may not be true, but you weren't there to hear it. Instead of responding to the quote from the PTA president (and possibly incurring wrath), it's better to say, "I can't respond to that, but the district is meeting the needs of middle school students by bringing in mentors and tutors to work with them after school." To further your credibility, you could add, "We're aware of the issues at the middle

EXHIBIT 4.9. Burnt Hills-Ballston Lake Central School District Key Talking Points
SOURCE: Burnt Hills-Ballston Lake Central School District; used by permission.

C. Key Talking Points

Themes for selling the referendum to the public

1. **The bond will cost residents very little.** Residents will receive $13 million in school improvements for a very modest cost. The increased cost to the average homeowner will be only $2-$19 per year.

2. **The District's 20-year history of maintaining our buildings through this process has been very successful.** We have a proven track record of following through on these promises. We have had no tax increases for major renovations for the past 20 years. Renovating our facilities in 5-year increments has allowed us both to plan ahead and to address problems before they grow more costly.

3. **The bond issue is a reflection of what BH-BL residents want for their schools and their children.** The Renovations Committee that selected and recommended these projects included a wide cross section and a majority of BH-BL residents and parents. The bond issue also reflects community values of excellent educational programs at a modest cost.

4. **The bond issue represents a unique opportunity to pay for higher state graduation requirements and other mandates with a higher rate of state aid.** Recognizing that doing more for students will cost school districts more, the state is temporarily offering to pay a higher percentage of the cost of building renovations and construction. We are required to provide more laboratory science for high school pupils, and it would be foolish not to take advantage of the current opportunity to have the state pay for 84% of these and other renovation needs.

5. **Ignoring these needs and doing nothing is not an alternative.** Many projects are mandated or will result in higher costs down the road if they are not addressed in a timely fashion. Most of our high school science labs were build in 1957. Renovating these and other needed facilities will never be any cheaper than it is today.

6. **Some renovations projects will not only pay for themselves very quickly but will also reduce our operating costs.** The lighting and communications projects could start saving us money within 2 years.

7. **Many school facilities do double duty and are used by other community organizations as well.** Our schools and playing fields are community gathering places used by many nonschool organizations. This means not only that high-use facilities like the high school cafeteria and auditorium are subject to a lot of wear and tear, but that renovating them will benefit many organizations beyond just the schools.

school level and are looking at more creative ways to address them," and then state what they are. If the questions are leading or if a reporter is fishing with vague questions, don't bite!

B. Don't allow a reporter to put words into your mouth. *Warning signs:* When you hear a reporter begin with, "Wouldn't you say" or "Don't you think," be careful with your response.

C. Correct misinformation. Do not assume that, on any given day when a reporter is given the assignment of covering a board of education meeting, she or he will completely grasp discussion items. A reporter who has just been handed an assignment for that day may have to cover a story with little or no background information. If the reporter has incorrect information, take the time to educate and then communicate in clear, concise terms. Some educational issues are complex to the layperson, and if beat reporters have never covered education, they could spend an inordinate amount of time asking background information. Again, this is when a fact sheet comes in handy.

10. *When distributing press releases or media advisories, don't play favorites with the media.* You will develop credibility by being fair with all. When planning a press conference, make sure all the media are invited, including those with a specific audience, such as Hispanic newspapers and television and radio stations. If you live in an area with a large Hispanic population, many of whom may not read the daily newspaper, you may be missing an important group of people who need to hear your message. Make sure that school publications are also available in Spanish and that translators are available at events.

11. *Take every opportunity, even under the most adverse circumstances, to deliver a positive message when dealing with the media.*

WNYT reporter Elaine Houston believes that every school will eventually have problems. "Society reflects it," she says. "But, if you're consistently doing more positive things, when something bad does happen, the general public will realize you're not the worst school in the world—especially if you handle a bad situation in a positive light."

Other Considerations

At the beginning of a school year, when staff development sessions are scheduled, include a media workshop and invite reporters or assignment editors to participate. This helps train administrators, the superintendent, and board members in how to handle the media and interviews. A good way to anticipate how the media may respond to a situation is by talking with them.

The benefit is twofold: (a) educators have a better understanding of what the media expect, and (b) it opens communication. It is much easier to call an assignment editor by name at a local television station after you have met her or him. The media will know whom to contact when calling the school the next time. Both groups can better grasp procedures.

WNYT's Television News Director S. Paul Conti and news anchor Ed Dague have participated in seminars with school districts on various issues. Schools present a situation to the team and then ask how the television station is apt to respond as if it would be covered. "They want to know so that they can better understand how to deal with it," said Conti.

Participating in a mock interview is a good way to experience how questions are generated (especially if the person asking the questions is a reporter), what techniques are used by reporters, and how to control the interview. KTVN-TV Channel 2 Reno has conducted mock media scenarios with the Nevada Department of Education, and related panel discussions for the local chapter of the Public Relations Society of America.

BOCES Public Information Specialist Paul Knittel has conducted a workshop using video in the Schenectady school district. He now conducts workshops with school officials in which the first half deals with the media in a crisis situation. He has brought a television news anchor and newspaper editor as part of the presentation. In addition, he does similar workshops at the State University of New York at Albany and the College of Saint Rose for school personnel working on their administrator's certificate.

Knittel emphasizes three main points in his workshops:

1. *Being prepared:* Understand how the media work (e.g., deadlines, assignment editors, knowledge level of reporters) and have the facts and no more than three speaking (message) points. "Speaking points are those items that you want to have quoted," said Knittel. "Then repeat them, repeat them, repeat them."

2. *Having confidence:* Know the situation, and know what the reporter is looking for (an angle). "Don't let the reporter's questions drive the interview. Be proactive and tell the reporter what you think is important and why and keep going back to it," he said. "Control the direction and message instead of the reporter controlling it by the questions asked."

3. *Finding something positive to say about the school/district in every situation:* "We had a popular music teacher die in a crash caused by another driver who was DWI," Knittel explained. "We focused on the crisis management team and how well they were working with students and staff."

Finally, consider joining the local chapters of either the National School Public Relations Association or the Public Relations Society of America. Both groups are great sources for networking and public relations/media tips.

5

Crisis Communications: Schools in Turmoil

A young girl throws her head back in silent agony as another teen tries to comfort her in vain. The headline below the photograph reads "Teen gunmen kill 25 in 'suicide attack.' " That photo was on the front page of *The Reno Gazette Journal* on April 21, 1999, which described the carnage at a Littleton, Colorado, high school—less than 1 year after 15-year-old Kipland Kinkel walked into Thurston High School in Springfield, Oregon, and opened fire on a packed high school lunchroom, leaving 2 students dead and 22 injured (see Exhibit 5.1).

For Cherie Kistner, the Colorado incident unleashed an emotional turmoil that has been with her for the past year. As the communications supervisor for the Springfield Public Schools, she was a core member of a multijurisdictional crisis communications team that dealt with the aftermath of Kinkel's assault. At the time of the incident, she says, she was operating in a "crisis mode" and didn't have time to think about the images released to the world. But Littleton changed that.

"We were so entrenched in what we were doing at the time, we didn't see how the stories were played out in the media. We weren't the end product. We were simply churning out information," she said. "It wasn't until I saw the news about the Littleton shooting that the full force of it hit. It was like standing outside and watching what happened at Thurston. Emotionally and psychologically, I cried for the first time."

Kistner first heard about the Thurston High School event as she was driving to work on May 21, 1998, and listening to the morning radio talk show. Immediately, she drove to the school, where the fire department's public information officer met her. Within minutes of the first emergency call, local news teams arrived. Television satellite trucks and news vans littered the area around Thurston High School, Springfield-area hospitals, and city hall shortly thereafter. "We immediately began working with the media," Kistner explained. "I worked with other school administrators in creating a list of the injured and began talking with parents. That became my role at the scene." While triage was set up at Thurston High School to treat the injured, a crisis information center was set up at city hall where all further communications were referred.

School violence has increased. With it comes media coverage. From CNN to the BBC, news of the Littleton incident filled the airwaves. No longer is violence the stomping grounds for big-city schools. It is striking in the most unlikely places, where doors are still left open at night. Even the best of schools cannot prevent the inevitable. Hall monitors, surveillance cameras, metal detectors, and school police may deter violence, but it can still happen in any community and in any school.

EXHIBIT 5.1. Front Page Headline of *The Oregonian*, May 23, 1998

Saturday, May 23, 1998

Sunrise Edition

Portland, Oregon 35¢

The Oregonian

THE LARGEST NEWSPAPER IN THE PACIFIC NORTHWEST

THE SPRINGFIELD SCHOOL SHOOTING

Struggling with the anguish

■ **THE SUSPECT:** *Kipland Kinkel appears docile when charged with aggravated murder*

■ **THE STUDENTS:** *Hundreds meet to cope with the aftermath of the school shooting*

By DANA TIMS, MAXINE BERNSTEIN and J. TODD FOSTER
of The Oregonian staff

EUGENE — The meek and subdued Kipland P. Kinkel who faced a Lane County judge Friday could not have presented a starker contrast to the bullet-spraying killer accused of the nation's largest school shooting.

With shoulders slumped and his trim, auburn hair barely touching his ears, the 15-year-old Thurston High School freshman could have been just another mischievous teenager in trouble at school. Instead, he heard his name used in connection with a crime that has shocked the nation: the aggravated murders Thursday of his parents and two classmates and the wounding of 22 students.

The carnage was compounded Friday by news that Kinkel might have tried to booby trap his home for deputies retrieving his parents'

Police examining the residence in a heavily wooded area 10 miles east of Springfield had to abandon it for a second time Friday afternoon after finding a fifth bomb. Earlier, Eugene and state police bomb squad members discovered and neutralized two sophisticated homemade bombs that contained timing devices, electrical circuitry and detonators. They also found two pipe bombs and a number of smaller explosives.

The discoveries occurred just after deputies removed the body of Faith Kinkel, 57. Stunned police said they thought they had seen everything during two horrific days.

"It's extraordinary," said Lane County Sheriff Jan Clements. "It's absolutely unbelievable to those of us who think rationally and understand what society is supposed to be all about.

"What's remarkable is looking all that up to a 15-year-old," Clements said.

The bodies of William Kinkel, 59, and his wife were found in different rooms in the family's rustic, three-story wooden chalet. There was no sign of struggle or neighborhood reports of gunfire, although both died of bullet wounds, authorities said.

At Thurston High, where 400 students had gathered before class Thursday, evidence recovered from Kinkel's backpack made it clear that the boy who had so many dark places in his life had been out to harm many, many more of his classmates.

Police retrieved several fully loaded, 50-round ammunition clips and a military-style knife from the backpack. They also found assorted loose ammunition, some of which spilled onto the tiled cafeteria floor when six students tackled Kinkel.

Firing from the hip, with the barrel pointed slightly upward, Kinkel exhausted the .22-caliber semiautomatic Ruger rifle he persuaded his father to let him buy with money earned from household chores.

Please turn to SHOOTING, Page A15

Above: Lane County sheriff's deputies escort Kipland P. Kinkel, 15, into a Lane County courtroom in Eugene on Friday. Kinkel was arraigned on charges of aggravated murder stemming from a shooting spree Thursday at Thurston High School.

PAUL KITIGAKI JR./The Oregonian

What police are finding in the Kinkel home

Since Thursday morning, authorities have been searching the home where Kip Kinkel lived. They have found an array of explosive devices as well as the bodies of his parents.

The bodies
■ The bodies of William and Faith Kinkel were found in separate rooms of the living area.

In crawl space:
■ **Four bombs:** two with electronic timing devices and two crude pipe bombs. Chemicals that could be used to make explosives.
■ **Fireworks**

Found throughout the house:
■ A fifth bomb
■ Two 155 mm howitzer canisters
■ One hand grenade
■ Detailed bomb making instructions, some of it apparently fetched from the Internet

Bomb disposal unit

MOLLY SWISHER/The Oregonian

Different response likely in other counties

After gun arrests, more scrutiny is the norm

BY ASHBEL S. GREEN, LAURA TRUJILLO and STEVE JONES
of The Oregonian staff

Springfield police were entirely within their discretion to release Kipland P. Kinkel to his parents Wednesday after arresting him for having a gun at school.

But in any other large county in Oregon, it probably wouldn't have happened that way.

Police in Clackamas, Washington, Multnomah and Linn counties, for example, rarely decide whether to release juvenile gun offenders, par-

ticularly if the arrest occurred in school. Instead, they routinely refer such offenders to county juvenile counselors, who are specially trained to spot the hidden potential for violence.

"That's the general rule," said Jason Carlile, Linn County district attorney and president of the Oregon District Attorneys Association. "That's generally how it would happen in Linn County, especially in a felony."

If juvenile counselors find proba-

Please turn to WHY, Page A13

EXHIBIT 5.2. Washoe County School District Sample Planning Document for a Crisis Communications Plan

SOURCE: Washoe County School District; used by permission.

WASHOE COUNTY SCHOOL DISTRICT
SCHOOL BOARD POLICIES

CRISIS PLANNING/MANAGEMENT

The Board of Trustees directs the Superintendent to develop and implement an organized plan to deal with any crisis that may arise in an attendance center or other work location. The administration and staff must have a plan on file in each work site, and a copy of the plan will be filed with the Superintendent. Staff will be trained in the implementation of the building crisis plan. All such plans will be approved by the Crisis Management Team. As necessary, students and parents will be informed about the details of any approved crisis plan.

All such plans shall include the following elements:

A. A staff training component

B. An emergency organizational structure detailing the chain of command and specific areas of staff responsibility

C. A communications and notification procedure for both district offices and other governmental entities

D. A process to periodically test the plan and conduct appropriate drills

E. Procedures to resume normal operations following an emergency event

---

Violence is just one crisis a school may be forced to handle. Prior to the Springfield shooting, Kistner had dealt with a sexual harassment claim against a coach and a potential teacher strike, all within the 3 years she's been with the district.

Schools have reported a fifth grader attempting suicide over poor grades, high school teachers charged with molesting students, elementary students playing with loaded guns on the bus to school, a principal being arrested for drunk driving, bomb threats, and the sudden accidental death of a beloved teacher. How well a school is prepared to handle the crisis will affect coverage in the media.

A crisis communications plan should be incorporated into any school's or district's overall communications plan (see Exhibit 5.2). It helps make a disastrous situation more manageable and builds on the district's credibility with its potentially affected interests (PAIs). First, look to the school district's public information office. If a plan is not in place, contact the Public Relations Society of America at (212) 995-2230 or *http://www.prsa.org/* for a chapter near you, or the nearest National School Public Relations Association chapter at (301) 519-0496 or *http://www.nspra.org/entry/htm* to get a sample of one.

The Washoe County School District operates under a Code 33 crisis plan (see Exhibit 5.3 for a page of the plan) as required by district policy at every school. It requires the school to go on "lock down" in case of an emergency, and it keeps everyone locked in their rooms and on campus unless the emergency is a fire or some other event that would require students and faculty to leave their rooms.

EXHIBIT 5.3. Washoe County School District Crisis Communications Team Procedures
SOURCE: Washoe County School District; used by permission.

Any member of the team can call a meeting.

If a team member calls and requests a meeting, the following procedures will be followed:

1. The member will call the Director of Student Support Services, Director of Communications, or Chief of School Police and advise them of a "Code 33."

2. Student Support Services, Communications, and School Police will notify all of the members of the Crisis Communication Team and instruct them to respond to the West Conference Room of the Administration Building. If the Administration Building is not available they should be advised to respond to Vaughn Middle School. The appropriate codes for the pager are:

    33-1   Administration Building (West Conference Room)

    33-2   Vaughn Middle School

3. All resources will be utilized to contact members of the Crisis Communication Team: home phone, office, pager, cellular phone, etc. If the person is not available, ask the person you are speaking with how you might reach the person. Get the name of the person you are talking with, or leave a message on the answering machine, of a Code 33 in progress and where to respond. If a member is contacted by pager, a 33-1 or 33-2 will appear on the pager, depending upon the designated location of the meeting.

4. Student Support Services will be the "Command Center" for the emergency.

5. All police officers are to keep an accurate log of their actions for a report that will be due at the conclusion of the incident.

After the Littleton, Colorado, incident, the district met with a committee of administrators, school police, and principals to review the code. The schools were asked to practice a "Code Red," or "Code 33" drill. In addition, Superintendent James Hager met with administrators, local law enforcement agency representatives, and local government representatives on how the entities could work together in the event of a shooting/bombing incident and how they could share information and identify ahead of time any students needing help. The hope is to get those students counseling to prevent drastic actions. As a final step, the members of the group formed a task force to iron out details of shared emergency event responsibilities and profiling/counseling of troubled youths.

If you are in the position of creating a crisis communications plan as a school administrator, here are steps to follow:

1. *Anticipate.* No one wants to imagine the worst-case scenario, but invariably a crisis will probably occur at some point in an educator's professional life. Do not think "It can't happen here," or you will be doing a huge disservice to your school and community. Be proactive. Solicit input from parents, teachers, and students. Asking for help in creating a plan before an event occurs builds on a bank of trust with the community (The Bleiker Lifepreserver).

(Text continues on page 79)

Strategies of a Public Information Response

1. Assemble a Team

The makeup of members depends on the situation. Role is to enable the organizations involved to focus on their tasks while team members deal with the barrage of phone calls, not only from the media, but from frantic community members, and from community members offering to help. This team should provide a "clearing house" for all information.

In Springfield, we had a core team of three public information officers as this was a multijurisdictional response between the city, the school district, and the county. Each hospital and neighboring cities joined our team. For district-only incidents, the team may consist of cabinet members (for negotiations); or the principal, the counselor, the teacher, and public information staff. Public information staff from all agencies met throughout the day and night for four days. When not physically together, we were in touch via fax, phone, e-mail, etc. and remain in touch today.

2. Control the Flow of Information

In large-scale crises, an immediate response—even if it's a prepared statement—acknowledging the incident occurred is the best route. A slow or no response might be viewed and reported as apparent guilt, a cover-up, etc. This could be as simple as a printed statement to the media or a letter to parents.

This act on your part leads to accurate reports in the media—reduces the chances of public pandemonium. In Springfield, once we were able to begin giving short snippets to the media, people knew they could stay tuned to their radio or their television set to get accurate, up-to-date information. This probably reduced the number of calls and visitors to the school.

Gather the facts, determine the impacts, identify necessary options, and assign responsibilities.

Set clear boundaries early, if necessary, and stick to them! Our school policy: no intrusions during the day. Once you stray, it's nearly impossible to get back.

Select spokespeople—Announce their availability. Announce if they will attend press conferences, etc. Joint briefings for spokespeople (the superintendent, the police chief, the sheriff, hospital managers, the DA) before press conferences are very helpful. IMPORTANT: Controlled information flow depends on sticking to the single-voice philosophy. This does not mean only one person talks, but coordinated efforts allow officials from each area to speak about their area of expertise. In a multijurisdictional situation, don't endeavor to answer questions not pertinent to your area.

Create talking points—so all speakers have same information and are giving consistent message.
BE CAREFUL: It's a tricky situation when a criminal act is involved.

EXHIBIT 5.4. Continued

3. Set Up an Information Center

This center should be a place that coordinates your efforts. If it's a school-based crisis, move AWAY FROM SCHOOL. Make it known to the community where they can get their information. Notify the media (or crowd) as to when to expect more information; tell them when the next update will occur.

In the district, this can be the personnel director's office during negotiations, the superintendent's office, or the principal's office. Depending on the situation, however, it provides for a common working space and common goals. This further enables you to maintain control of the situation—control of the information.

In Springfield, we prepared joint agency news releases; all information was on one release. For negotiations, finance, benefits, and instruction could all have input into documents we produced.

Triage phone calls appropriately; set priorities; don't hesitate to let callers know your priorities, which will give them a general idea as to when you'll respond to their request.

Plan how to manage the media at the events that follow the crises.

Set up **status boards** for releasing updated information.

Your ultimate communications goal is to maintain credibility and provide accurate information in a timely manner. Credible, credible, credible—that's the bottom line.

Don't chase rumors—report the facts. If you're all in one room, it makes verification convenient. (Death of a student announced at a church service was reported to us. We served as the central point for the rest of our agency's operations.)

As soon as you run out of new information, close down the joint information center. We still collaborated for a few more days, when the need arose—meaning when new information needed to be shared.

4. Communicate as Quickly as Possible

Communicate within minutes or hours of the event. Provide regular briefings on the status of the crisis.

This isn't to say to always jump right on the situation; there are times when a delay is helpful—but there are also times when a delay leaves you playing catch-up. Make sure all members of your team are informed in a timely manner—preferably before hearing it on the television or radio news.

Regular briefings and official statements give the news form and structure.

Provide a list of names and telephone numbers for contact information (daily if appropriate).

EXHIBIT 5.4. Continued

5. **Work With the Media as a Partner, Not the Enemy.**

Don't forget: *You also need the media* to communicate with your community at large. ALL groups need the information in one fell swoop. In a large-scale event, it isn't possible to hold a variety of informational sessions for special-interest groups.

Don't forget, however, you still must **maintain sensitivity to victims, staff, parents,** etc. For example, Springfield released the names of injured students to the crowd at the high school first, not to the media. We didn't want parents to hear on television that their child was hurt before they heard it from an official.

We needed to **relay important information** about telephone numbers, memorials, vigils, patient information, etc. Our daily newspaper ran an excellent "how you can help" column daily for several weeks.

It is not your role to censor the media or to determine how they present information; they'll make or break themselves in a large-scale crisis situation. In exchange, you are able to tell them what your expectations are—that you expect coverage that is fair, accurate, and balanced.

Lay the ground work for understanding; in our situation, we were able to say at any given time, this is what we know now; this is what we don't know (e.g., not being able to identify the bodies). Because we were timely, accurate, honest, and authoritative, we earned the media's respect and cooperation. Don't be afraid to set clear boundaries early and stick to them.

An important note: Don't get caught up in the glamour of national media—it gets old. And be prepared if you stray from the one-voice principle noted earlier. Once you let them in, they keep coming. And be careful to always present your united front and be on guard; the media, like any other group, will look for the weak link.

—Cherie Kistner, Springfield Public Schools

Look to your school district first for emergency action plans and then at building-level plans. Is there a communications component? An integral part of handling a crisis well is swift, accurate information. If plans do not exist, assemble a core advisory group consisting of police, fire, medical, city, county, and school district representatives to help create one. Determine who the key contacts are in an emergency; create a plan and distribute copies to all team members. Schedule a staff development day at the beginning of the school year for a mock disaster drill with other agencies, and focus on communication.

In Springfield, Oregon, the district created a crisis plan in two phases before the shooting incident (see Exhibit 5.4). According to Cherie Kistner, the first phase was reactionary, involving fire, police, and emergency medical service (EMS) units; the second phase was mental preparation. A school psychologist from the district assembled a team of administrators, a risk manager, and a security officer.

As the lead communicator in a crisis, you will be the main source of information. The media will defer to you as a guide to accessing what they need: background information, legal issues, school policies and procedures. If you do not know the answer to something, you should quickly and easily be able to contact someone who does. Having fact sheets available on the school/district will quickly and easily address general questions.

A plan should first address the immediate safety concerns of the issue and then the steps necessary to communicate it to a school's PAIs, as well as the media. Crises vary in magnitude, but two things are key to the outcome: (a) the safety and welfare of the school community and (b) the immediate notification of parents.

For Example: A fifth grader carries a gun on a school bus on the way to school. He plays with it as if it's a toy, showing his friends. The bus driver immediately notifies the principal on reaching the school. The police are contacted, and the student is called to the principal's office. The gun, which is real, is taken from the student, and the student is taken to police headquarters. The principal's main concern is with the student's safety and that of the general school community. The school psychologist is brought in to work with the student's classmates and to explain the situation to them. Calls are placed to the student's family. The principal immediately drafts a letter to be sent home to all parents, explaining the situation and what steps will be taken to handle the immediate concerns of the student body. The school's no-tolerance policy on violence and guns is reiterated.

As the first and best source of information, you want to quell rumors and misinformation before the news is broadcast. At the same time, the media begin calling because they have picked up over a scanner that an elementary student has been arrested. They want to come to school to videotape the student's classroom. As principal, you realize that doing this will disrupt and upset the other students even further. Instead, you work with the police and the media and determine a site that is least disruptive to the school community, such as the police station. Make yourself available for comment there and make sure your information is accurate and coincides with the police report.

2. *Prepare.* After creating a crisis communications plan, put it into action. Letting it sit on the shelf will do no good once a crisis occurs. Mike Moskovitz, public information officer for Lane County, Oregon, was involved with the Springfield incident. He has 28 years in the news, broadcasting, and public relations. He says that each agency involved in the Springfield shooting had separate crisis communications plans but no time to read them and then put them into action. Because each agency had experienced public information officers, team crisis coordination worked smoothly despite the situation. Not every school or district will have a public information officer (see Exhibit 5.5), so it is best to work with local resources (police, fire, medical institutions, and school district personnel) to create scenarios to explore the best course of action. Define roles so that all players in a crisis situation know who to turn to with little duplication of efforts.

EXHIBIT 5.5. A Page From the Washoe County Emergency Management Plan
SOURCE: Washoe County Emergency Management; used by permission.

PUBLIC INFORMATION OFFICER

■ Responsibility: Developing and releasing information about the emergency to the news media, emergency personnel, and to other appropriate jurisdictions, agencies and organizations.

The Public Information Officer may have assistants as needed, and the assistants may also represent other affected and/or assisting jurisdictions, agencies and organizations. The Public Information Officer may establish a Joint Information Center with other assisting and/or affected jurisdictions, agencies and organizations to create a single point of contact, and facilitate coordinated and combined public information activities.

■ Basic Tasks:
  ■ Determine, from the EOC Director, if there are any limits on information release.
  ■ Develop material for use in media briefings.
  ■ Obtain EOC Director's approval for media releases.
  ■ Inform media and conduct media briefings.
  ■ Arrange for tours and other interviews or briefings that may be required.
  ■ Obtain media information that may be useful to emergency planning.
  ■ Maintain current information summaries and/or displays on the emergency and provide information on status of emergency to assigned personnel.
  ■ Participate in and help coordinate the operation of a Joint Information Center as needed.

■ Regional Coordination Considerations/Tasks:
  ■ Responsible for satisfying the need for regional information gathering
  ■ Operates a Joint Information Center (JIC)
  ■ Provides summary information from jurisdiction, agency and incident public information officers
  ■ Identifies local sources for additional information

LIAISON

■ Responsibility: The contact for the personnel assigned to the emergency by assisting or cooperating jurisdictions, agencies and organizations (other than those in direct operational assignments or those involved in a Unified Management).

The Liaison may have assistants as needed, and the assistants may also represent assisting jurisdictions, agencies or organizations.

■ Basic Tasks:
  ■ The contact point for the interface between the EOC and Agency Representatives from other involved jurisdictions, agencies and organizations.
  ■ Maintain a list of assisting and cooperating jurisdictions, agencies, organizations and Agency Representatives.

Review past crisis situations to see what did and did not work. Evaluate your resources within the school to see how they can be applied to a crisis. For example, Thurston High School has a Health Occupation Students of America (HOSA) program. The group works with the community on EMS disaster drills at the school. When the shooting occurred, the students knew how to respond. According to Kistner, by the time emergency responders got to the school, many of the HOSA students were already working with teachers to help the injured.

Get all important telephone numbers on one handy sheet of paper, including police emergency and the school's attorney. That way, you won't have to scramble when pressed for information or contacts.

The Crisis Communicators Council in Reno, Nevada, meets once a month so that, in the event of an emergency, everyone understands protocol and what steps to take. The council consists of the school district; airport, medical, casino, and public relations agencies; and county and city agency members.

According to Washoe County Community Relations Director Kathy Carter, the council began as a loose-knit support group for public information officers. "Now we're looking at training exercises and not just sharing stories," she said. "We familiarize ourselves with other people, their phone numbers and crisis plans," said Christopher Good, City of Reno public communication coordinator and a council member. "In the event of an emergency that may involve the county, I know exactly how to get hold of Kathy Carter and draft her to help me. Or, if an emergency involves the school district, I can immediately call their communications office and I don't have to introduce myself. The contact has already been made."

The Federal Aviation Administration (FAA) requires the Airport Authority of Washoe County to conduct mock emergency preparedness drills every several years. In 1999, in conjunction with the city of Reno, the airport authority conducted a mock broken-propeller-aircraft disaster exercise. Many members of the Crisis Communications Council participated in the event, including Sonya Gordon, communications specialist for the Washoe County School District. She played the role of a National Public Radio reporter, a task not unfamiliar to her because she has been a reporter for the *Reno Gazette Journal* and the *Daily Reporter* in Columbus, Ohio, and a radio reporter for WFOR-FM in Hattiesburg, Mississippi.

"The beauty of an exercise like this is that you can identify any weaknesses in the plan before a disaster occurs," she said. "Any time there's a community disaster, it affects a school or district in some way. For example, an explosives factory blew up on the east side of town, resulting in a plume of possibly toxic substances that was released into the atmosphere. Although not directly related to a school, the direction of the wind was moving that cloud over to area schools. Because we were unsure of the content of the cloud, parents were concerned and we kept children in those schools indoors as a precaution until the 'all clear' sign was given."

According to Gordon, school officials learned how to work cooperatively with other agencies in the event of an emergency and to get the word out to parents through the media as soon as possible. When dealing with a crisis, appoint a lead spokesperson from each agency so that, regardless of the situation, each is speaking clearly and intelligently on the subject at hand. Credibility is achieved through the dissemination of accurate information where all the players adhere to the same principle.

Moskovitz writes in a *3CMA* article on the Springfield incident:

> Controlled information flow depends on sticking to a single source philosophy, that is, speaking with one voice. This does not mean only one person talks, but coordinated efforts allow officials from each area to speak about their area of expertise. Together all the information forms one coherent story that is free of contradiction, misinformation and rumors.

SOURCE: This article originally appeared in *3CMA News*, October 1998, and is extracted from above with permission of the City-County Communications and Marketing Association and Mike Moskovitz.

Kistner added, "Knowing each other and being prepared made a disaster situation more manageable. If we didn't know each other it would have hampered our efforts. Instead, it was natural and easy for us and there was a trust level in sharing information." With adequate planning, a crisis team can go into maximum overdrive with little confusion and smooth communication.

3. *Research.* Gather facts. Misinformation can damage even the best of efforts in a crisis situation. In the immediate wake of a crisis event, the media begin reporting an incident with few facts at hand. They are often responding to what is transmitted over police scanners. You are likely to deal with a community that will react in fear and anger. Imagine a parent at work hearing the news of the Littleton, Colorado, high school shooting and not knowing whether his child is safe or fatally injured. Or another parent reading in the newspaper that her child's math teacher has been suspended for suspected child molestation. Parents, teachers, and citizens demand immediate information, and they have a right to it.

As a public institution, the school is accountable, though not necessarily responsible, for every incident that happens there. Get the facts and report everything possible. Do not respond to media questions with "I think." State what you know, or find out and report back. Rumor control is an important part of managing a crisis. The media can latch onto skimpy information, and it can take on a life of its own. Even innocuous statements can run amok.

4. *Mobilize.* By 10 a.m. on the day of the Thurston High School shooting in Springfield, Oregon, a 13-member crisis communications team was in place. Said Moskovitz, "The team met throughout the crisis, into the nights, days, and weeks that followed. When not physically together, we stayed in constant touch via e-mails, faxes, and many phone calls." According to Moskovitz, the role of the team was to allow the organizations involved (school district, police and fire departments) to get on with the "operational aspects of the job devoid of media interference. We dropped our organizational egos. We worked for each other. We worked for the community."

On the basis of your crisis plan, you should already have a team of people to call in an emergency. From school building personnel to outside agencies, individuals should be assigned tasks to keep the situation under control—particularly communications. School police, counselors, teachers, and support staff should be familiar with emergency drills before a crisis hits. Once it does, they should move as one cohesive unit.

5. *Move and Deliver.* The situation in Springfield, Oregon, is a good example of how to control information while at the same time delivering timely, important messages to the media. Once an information center was set up at city hall, the crisis information team disseminated press releases twice a day.

"We took control," said Moskovitz. "We didn't operate as separate units, allowing the media to take over and show up at different locations demanding immediate attention. We sent press releases out from one place twice a day. If the media wanted the information, they had to show up at the information center."

In keeping the information exact and all agencies up to speed on the progress of the case, each agency's representative was at the center. As press releases were drafted, Cherie Kistner, Mike Moskovitz, and other agency representatives added relevant details to one press release. Everyone was operating from the same perspective, and the media got accurate information.

Although not all crisis situations will require the magnitude of coordination the Springfield incident did, one key school/district person should take the communications lead in a school/district event. Usually, that responsibility falls to an administrator if a public information officer is not available. In a crisis, there is only time to act, and training, good information, and a strong support group will allow for decisions to be smooth, actions to be more manageable, and the communications to be precise.

After 4 intensive days of working with the media, Mike Moskovitz looks back and realizes that although the crisis at Thurston High School was handled as well as could be expected, he did learn some things. He wrote in the *3CMA* newsletter:

> Looking back, there were things we should have done or could have done better: We should have monitored the news to find out who is writing or saying what. Yet we were so overwhelmed with media requests, we did not have time to thoroughly read papers or monitor broadcast news accounts. We should have assigned a volunteer to handle that important task.
>
> We should have controlled rumors, but did not have the time. Rumors always give the impression of truth. The best defense against rumors is to keep getting out frequent, high quality information. While we caught and cleared up major rumors, we ignored minor ones. We focused on what we knew as fact and got that out.

SOURCE: This article originally appeared in *3CMA News*, October 1998, and is reprinted here with permission of the City-County Communications and Marketing Association and Mike Moskovitz.

One rumor in particular could have had devastating results for the family of one of the victims. At a prayer vigil, one pastor mentioned, incorrectly, that one victim was on the verge of death or had died. Although Moskovitz was not present at the vigil, when he called a local television station later that night to check on an unrelated development, a reporter asked about the death.

"I literally stumbled across the rumor," he said. "I clarified the information and asked if the other television stations were present for the vigil as well. They were, so I called the other stations to clear the misinformation. The media feeds on one another and picks up information quickly. Had the friends or family of the student heard that information first, it would have been devastating."

> We should have had more sleep. In the first three days, I worked 60 hours. That is 20 hours a day. All of us were worn out and on the verge of grumpiness. Even in tragedy, we tried to keep our sense of humor to get through it all.
>
> I should not have assumed I could do it alone. The enormity of the situation was unbelievable. Sunday following the shooting, I worked alone to prepare a statement from the Sheriff's office. In those two short hours my pager and telephone went off 24 times. That is one interruption every five minutes. I struggled to get the release written.
>
> I should have done a better job in keeping my papers in order. With an overloaded clipboard full of telephone numbers, notes, to-do lists, releases, mug shots and handouts, my records system was a mess. It was not until day three that I got wise about putting items into folders organized in a portable file.
>
> We should have known the unexpected can happen at any time. We learned it really can happen here. Now we know it can happen anywhere.

SOURCE: This article originally appeared in *3CMA News*, October 1998, and is reprinted here with permission of the City-County Communications and Marketing Association and Mike Moskovitz.

6

Forming Partnerships in Communications

All the world is one.

> —Former First Lady of New York State, Matilda Raffa Cuomo,
> quoting her father, Charles

Within days of the 1997 New Year, Judith Simpson watched helplessly from a distance as the remains of the Partners in Education (PIE) office could barely be seen above the rushing Truckee River current. After a prolonged heavy snowfall, that Nevada river flooded its banks, wreaking havoc and causing millions of dollars in damage along its shoreline in Reno. "We lost our history. We had nothing left," said Simpson, coordinator of the nonprofit organization created by the Washoe County School District and the Greater Reno-Sparks Chamber of Commerce in Reno-Sparks, Nevada.

Located north of the river, the PIE facility houses staff, as well as a warehouse of donated items from local businesses that are available to district schools and personnel at no cost. Everything—including paper supplies, coffee mugs, videotapes, computers, and furniture—is there for the asking. With a total value of more than $700,000, Simpson said of the successful program, "Your trash is our treasure."

After the flood, only a glass table and a few metal cabinets remained. The power of one of their partnerships in particular, however, changed that. With 20 strong years of forging community relationships, Partners in Education didn't struggle too long. CBS affiliate KTVN-TV Channel 2 Reno is one partner that played a pivotal role. Within 6 weeks, PIE reopened its doors with an almost fully stocked warehouse. "Channel 2 followed us over a period of 6 weeks," said Simpson. "They were there when the bulldozers arrived. They did live news broadcasts from our location. It didn't take long to get the message out that we needed help, and the community responded."

Through a joint venture between the school district and the chamber of commerce, PIE has had enormous success in communicating its program. Not only do the staff publish their own newsletter, *A Slice of PIE*, and an annual report, but their business and community partners also act as sources of information through internal publications and the media.

Many schools are partnered with agencies that have their own public relations departments. In-house communications offices can generate company newsletters and have the workers to focus on pitching stories to the media. When done well, business/partnership communications convey the mission and goals of a school district and are not self-serving public relations with little or no support (see Exhibit 6.1).

According to Paula Sulinski, president of Third Street Marketing and Media Services, a public relations and marketing agency based in Detroit, Michigan, schools need to look to business and community partners to communicate school programs because letters sent home to parents and brochures simply aren't enough. Her involvement with the Fitzgerald School District in Warren, Michigan, helped bring visibility to a groundbreaking national pilot apprenticeship program among the district, Sears Automotive, and the Automotive Service Association in 1997. The program offered 500 to 1,000 high school students an opportunity to train with the Automotive Service Association (a network of auto dealers) and Sears Automotive. Components of the program included wages, a certificate from the Bureau of Apprenticeship and Training, journeyman status, and a degree from Macomb Community College as an option. "Business partners are training kids to become part of the real world," said Sulinski. "Schools need to let the community know what's happening through other resources."

The district contacted Sulinski to help launch the program 2 weeks prior to a ceremony celebrating the partnership. Because of her extensive background in broadcasting, she was able to pull off a strong public relations effort. Although the ceremony was not billed as a press conference, but rather as a coverage opportunity, the media responded. In addition to coverage on a local television station, articles ran in *Crain's Detroit Business* and *The Detroit News*.

"There are so many ways you can pitch a story like the Sears apprenticeship program," explained Sulinski. "It was about education, business, and the automotive industry. It was a photo opportunity too. Everyone from students to business leaders was available for the media to interview at one time and in one place."

The school's program was publicly heralded for its innovation. Parents and students unfamiliar with the program called for more information or to enroll. "The press coverage showed that schools are being responsive to the community's need for trained employees for these businesses," said Sulinski. "It also helped bring other companies into the program who were initially resistant."

Media coverage did more than just showcase the program. It lent credibility. After the articles ran, Sulinski received a call from an Oakland County, Michigan, school administrator to see how she could help the district get involved in a similar program. The school administrator had been sent a copy of *The Detroit News* article from a Chrysler executive in charge of funding educational programs who wanted to do the same thing. "The more you can do for a reporter, the better," said Sulinski. "Play all aspects of the story. Look at what the school partnership offers. Star power is certainly one way to get publicity. It gets attention."

Star power helped build one of the strongest and most visible school partnerships in New York. In 1986, New York Governor Mario Cuomo asked his wife, Matilda, to do him a favor. Appalled by a New York State Department of Education report that indicated an unacceptably high dropout rate in the state, Cuomo asked Matilda, a mother of five and a former teacher, to help "stem the tide" of student dropouts. Not only did she step up to the plate, but she's also a Hall of Famer for advocating mentoring and school partnerships. She created the New York State Mentoring Program, the nation's first statewide one-to-one school-based mentoring program. And wherever Matilda Cuomo went, the media were sure to follow. "Back in 1987, no one knew what I was talking about," she said. "Mentoring? What's that? But in 12 years as part of the New York State Mentoring Program, we reached 10,000 kids. By the time the program ended, everyone knew about mentoring."

When Cuomo first started the New York State Mentoring Program, she volunteered to become a mentor to Ely Delgado, an elementary student in the City School District of Albany, New York. Through her work,

EXHIBIT 6.1. Airport Authority of Washoe County *Airport Flyer,* Winter 1999
SOURCE: Airport Authority of Washoe County; used by permission.

Community News from the
Airport Authority of Washoe County

WINTER 1999

The Airport Authority Of Washoe County Welcomes New Executive Director

On November 30, 1998, the Board of Trustees chose Krys T. Bart, A.A.E. to lead the AAWC into the next century. She has become responsible for providing aviation services and facilities at both Reno/Tahoe International Airport and Reno Stead Airport.

I am delighted to be here in Reno," said Bart. "I am honored the Board of Trustees had the confidence in me, and am looking forward to becoming acquainted and working with the staff. I know we are faced with many challenges, and I am excited to go to work!"

Managing airports is nothing new to Bart. Preceding her appointment at Reno/Tahoe, Bart was the Assistant Director of Aviation at San Jose International Airport. Her responsibilities included the day-to-day management of California's fourth largest airport, serving 11 million passengers annually and operating with an annual budget of $145 million.

For five years prior to her assignment in San Jose, Bart held the position of Assistant Airports Director and was responsible for day-to-day management responsibilities for both Fresno Air Terminal and the Chandler Downtown Airport, a general aviation reliever airport.

Prior to entering the aviation industry, Krys was heavily involved in the development of real estate property, with over 15 years' experience in all phases of commercial, residential and industrial land development. During that time, she was a principal in a real estate consulting firm providing development feasibility analyses and project management to public and private clients. She attended the University of Toledo and graduated with honors from California State University, Fresno, where she received a bachelors degree in Environmental Science.

As an Accredited Airport Executive, Bart serves as a member of the Board of Directors of the American Association of Airport Executives (AAAE). She is also a Certified Airport Executive with the Southwest Chapter of the American Association of Airport Executives (SWAAAE).

In July, 1994, Bart was the first woman to receive the "Aviation Excellence Award" from the SWAAAE and, in July, 1996, she was installed as the first woman president in the 50 year history of the organization. She has also received commendations from the United States Marine Corps, the U.S. Forest Service and the Airport Fire Rescue and Fire Fighting Group for her support of their aviation related needs.

Bart is actively involved in professional and community organizations. She has been on the Board of Directors of the San Jose International Airport Rotary, past-member of the Board of Directors of the Fresno Women's Network, the United Way of Fresno County and Valley Children's Hospital Development Foundation. In 1992, she was a finalist for the Fresno Business and Professional Woman of the Year.

Krys T. Bart, A.A.E.

In This Issue

86

EXHIBIT 6.1. Continued

(2)

1999 & The Challenges Ahead

The new year rings in resolutions for Reno/Tahoe International Airport. Air service development and customer satisfaction will be a priority, and 1999 will bring us many challenges.

For one, it is no secret that our passenger traffic is down about 1% for 1998. This can be attributed to a number of factors including a reduction of service by Reno Air.

The acquisition of Reno Air by American Airlines has also created concern in the community that we will lose valuable air service. However, a year end meeting with American Airlines President & CEO Donald Carty, and a delegation led by Senator Bryan accompanied by Governor Guinn, Mayor Griffin, Board of Trustees Chairman Bruce, and Trustee Menchetti along with other business leaders, assured Reno/Tahoe that American will not make any radical changes in the short term future. We will continue to make American aware of the benefits they can reap by maintaining a strong presence at Reno/Tahoe International.

So, in the meantime, we need to strive to be the best at what we do. Leaving the very best first and last impression for our air travelers, and focusing on first class customer service will make our success.

Let us also take this opportunity to recognize Richard Bennett, who served as the AAWC's Interim Executive Director from July to December 1998, and Miles Crafton, who served as Interim Director of Administration. Both have been instrumental in maintaining efficient operations, while continuing to focus on the future. Mr. Bennett will serve as the Interim Director of Administration while we search for a permanent replacement, and Mr. Crafton will return to his duties as Manager of Human Resources. Please join us in thanking them for a job well done.

We invite your comments and suggestions to make the AAWC a more efficient organization, and rich in quality customer service.

Wishing you all a healthy and prosperous New Year.

Swope Student Council

Partners In Education

The Airport Authority (AAWC) helped bring in the new school year (Fall 1998) with a $1,600 donation to its Partner In Education, Swope Middle School, which will upgrade the computers in the library. Internet access will soon be available to students as well. This will definitely help students get the latest research on a vast number of subjects.

The annual report on the status of the Swope-Airport Authority partnership was presented to AAWC employees at their October 29th meeting. This report was eloquently given by eighth grade students Alex Creekman and Chelsea Miller.

Over the holidays there was much collaboration and generosity between the AAWC and Swope Middle School. The Swope jazz band played at the AAWC's anniversary bash on November 12. During the months of November and December, AAWC employees and Swope students busily collected foods items for needy Swope families, and distributed by AAWC employees. Swope chorus, strings and band members brought holiday cheer and music to the airport terminal. The annual gingerbread contest/display was held in December and all proceeds from this display were donated to the Kids' Kottage, a safe haven for children in distressed home situations.

EVENTS TO LOOK FORWARD TO IN 1999:

February 19-26: Career Week at Swope
March 12: Job shadowing at the airport
August: Airport Authority golf tournament

PHOTO 6.1. Montessori Magnet School Student Kaleb Hogan, Albany, New York
SOURCE: Photograph by Joe Elario; used by permission.

Cuomo and Delgado have been featured on numerous television shows and in many publications, including the May 13, 1997, issue of *Family Circle* and in Cuomo's book *The Person Who Changed My Life.* Cuomo's goal was to help schools accomplish their mission to educate all students. She accomplished that by getting the media's attention. The attention fueled a stronger program and more mentoring volunteers.

"My father used to say, 'All the world is one,' which means we must step in to help students that are emotionally neglected. Mentoring helps build self-esteem, and it gets grades going," she said.

In 1995, a new administration eliminated the New York State Mentoring Program. Its phoenix was Mentoring USA, a nonprofit group that Cuomo founded and that is now operating throughout the United States and Italy. Companies such as Conair Corporation, AT&T, Bell Atlantic, Prudential, Kenneth Cole, and Nickelodeon have stepped forth to lend support—personally through mentoring, and by encouraging their employees to volunteer.

The PIE team also realizes that if the program is to continue to grow and further its mission to help all Washoe County School District students "in reaching their full potential, utilizing partnerships, community resources and volunteers to develop and implement diverse educational opportunities," then communications is key.

To that end, Judith Simpson and the PIE Board of Directors created a marketing plan (see Exhibit 6.2) that addresses organizational shortcomings and greater community recognition. With an eye toward positioning the program in the forefront of Washoe County citizens and businesses, the plan specifies that PIE staff will (a) provide a minimum of 10 articles per year for use in partners' newsletters, (b) provide a regular column in the chamber newsletter, and (c) highlight volunteer successes through media press promotions. Additionally, some of PIE's businesses have their own plans. The Reno Hilton dedicates one page of its Web site to Partners in Education (see Exhibit 6.3).

(Text continues on page 92)

EXHIBIT 6.2. PIE Marketing Plan
SOURCE: Partners in Education, Inc., 775-353-5533; used by permission.

PRIORITY: IMMEDIATE GOALS (by 1/1/99)	Responsibility	Time
Develop response card to be handed out at every speaking engagement to recruit volunteers	staff/WCSD	1 hour/***
Increase distribution of PIE newsletter to include PTA/PFA or other groups' officers and include each teacher involved with PIE	staff	10 hours/***
Provide semiannual report to members of corporation (chamber/WCSD), either in writing or in person on: A. Status of each program area and progress of each B. Progress in meeting strategic plans established C. Results of any quantitative/qualitative evaluations D. Feedback regarding needs and composition for new board members to ensure diversity and community representation E. Financial status and needs	staff/president	12-18 hours/year
Provide written marketing plan progress reports from staff to board meetings	staff	1 hour/mo.
Provide written committee reports to board meetings	chairs	1 hour/mo.
Establish staff and volunteer speakers bureau and schedule speaking engagements at least five times a month, particularly at schools, organizations/associations, businesses, service and professional clubs, and PTA/PFAs A. Use emotional appeal, successes to tell PIE story B. Share statistics C. Recognize worthy audience members D. Display logo at all engagements E. "Ask"	board recruit/volunteers	10 hours/mo.
Send a personal thank-you card to major volunteers/donors each year from the PIE president	president	1 hour/mo.
Communicate marketing goals and objectives to PIE staff through annual review by marketing chair with staff	marketing chair/staff	2 hours/year
Develop annual calendar and distribute to staff, board, corporate, and school members	staff	3 hours
PRIORITY: SHORT-TERM GOALS (by 1/1/00)	**Responsibility**	**Time**
Establish "round table" discussions to obtain ongoing feedback with the following: A. With key business partners at PIE location to (1) introduce partners to warehouse facility and (2) allow a forum for ongoing feedback B. With volunteers to provide thoughts on (1) how to better help them and (2) how to recruit additional volunteers C. Parents, teachers, and administrators from each school to (1) identify specific needs and (2) identify opportunities to improve relationship	staff/board	2 hours/12 times a year

EXHIBIT 6.2. Continued

PRIORITY: SHORT-TERM GOALS (by 1/1/00)	Responsibility	Time
Annual review of participation level by each school. Establish specific goals, maintenance, and expansion of participation. Develop list of schools to target each quarter.	staff	200 hours
Establish a regular media relations program through WCSD office of communications	WCSD	2 hours/mo.
Contact new businesses coming to the area through EDAWN for partnership opportunities	staff/volunteer	2 hours/mo.
Conduct annual retreat for board and staff including training in marketing responsibilities by board members	staff/board	6 hours/year
Conduct annual orientation by board volunteers and staff for all new board members	board	3 hours/year
Include marketing responsibilities in job description for board members	board	2 hours
PRIORITY: ONGOING AND ADDITIONAL LONG-TERM GOALS	**Responsibility**	**Time**
Provide at least 10 articles per year for business partners' employee newsletters	staff	20 hours
Recognize donors in annual report each year. Seek other ways to say thank you to partners	staff	20 hours***
Distribute weekly staff meeting minutes to appropriate partners	staff	weekly
Develop consistent promotional materials to promote PIE through use of the new logo and in accordance with national guidelines	staff/volunteers	ongoing***
Highlight individual volunteer success stories both in newsletter and in media press promotions	staff	2 hours/mo.
Incorporate a specific "ask" in all communication efforts	staff/volunteers	ongoing
Use fax/e-mail opportunities where possible and needed for immediate communication and/or feedback	staff/volunteers	ongoing
Establish a regular column from the PIE director in the newsletter and the WCSD *This Week*	E.D.	3 hours/mo.
Share success stories of PIE partners and individual volunteers in newsletter and media press promotions. Actively seek business and school "contributors" to the publication.	staff	2 hours/mo.
Ask each volunteer to recruit an additional volunteer annually through Committed to Kids program. Provide incentives.	volunteers	annually
Establish a mechanism for greater contact and feedback with parents	volunteers	9 hours/year
Establish a PIE Web site	volunteer/consultant	20 hours***
Develop a professional presentation through laptop/display projector for speakers bureau	staff/consultant	20-30 hours***

NOTE: ***Financial commitment required above staff/volunteer hours

EXHIBIT 6.3. Reno Hilton's PIE Web Page
SOURCE: Reno Hilton; used by permission.

The Reno Hilton Is A Partner in Education

The Reno Hilton was chosen by the Partners In Education organization as the Adopt-A-School partner for Vaughn Middle School in May 1998.

Partners in Education was established to strengthen the education experience for Washoe County School District Students through the creation and management of business and community/school programs and alliances.

The Adopt-A-School program helps students prepare for work by exposing them to different career opportunities and their educational requirements, increasing student motivation to look ahead and be prepared for the future, and increasing community understanding of the school system.

Some of the activities employees at the Reno Hilton have been involved with include:

1. Participation in the annual BBQ dinner for students who are entering 7th grade and their parents. We had fun flipping burgers and hotdogs and getting to know the students and faculty.

2. Participation in the school's annual assembly program, which included a presentation by cast members of the Aireus production who demonstrated humor, dance and gymnastics skills.

"While PIE has the history, credibility, staff, volunteer base, and a clear message, it can all be overridden in short order by communications failures," said Simpson. That concept holds true whether it's a school district in Reno, Nevada, or in upstate New York, where school and business alliances have been integrated throughout the state for many years.

Prior to the creation of the federal School-to-Work Opportunities Act in 1994, the City School District of Albany, New York, was steeped in school-to-work programs. Curt King was the school district coordinator for the School and Business Alliance (SABA), which operated for many years and built solid relationships between the business community and the district. In addition, Cuomo was a staunch supporter, and during that time, the New York State Mentoring Program was flourishing.

"Our purpose was to put businesses and schools together and have small, effective programs," said King. "SABA set up boards of business and education that gave them money to help determine how to best raise educational standards." The word got out and spread like fire. SABA's programs were popular with the Albany Colonie Chamber of Commerce, and it was promoted through in-house publications, breakfast meetings, public radio, and television. "The chamber was the key to our getting all the good press," King added.

Albany Medical Center was one of the first businesses to take part in a career explorations program with the City School District of Albany, before School-to-Work grant funds became available. Chris Urbano, a registered nurse and health explorations teacher at the district's Abrookin Vocational Technical Center, created the pilot program in 1994. The program later expanded to include the Veterans Hospital. Geared toward Albany High School seniors who demonstrated a keen interest in pursuing medical careers, the program quickly caught on. It received attention in the school district's publication, *Capital Education*; Albany Medical Center's *Center News* (see Exhibit 6.4); local newspapers; television news; and a special segment on *Spirit of Discovery*, the school district's news magazine show, which aired on the local public broadcasting station WMHT. The combined communications efforts got the attention of the New York State Education Department, which later videotaped one of Urbano's medical ethics discussions for broadcast to teachers throughout the state. "You need to go out and knock on doors to get the resources, the partnerships to build programs like this," she said. "They will fail if not promoted." Although the program was created a year before federal School-to-Work funding became available, "It clearly was a program that demonstrated school-to-work concepts," Urbano said.

Today, the district has four career explorations programs: criminal justice, finance, health, and education. Partners include College of Saint Rose; State University of New York at Albany; Albany Medical Center; family, civil, and police court; public defenders; the district attorney; Bell Atlantic; and Soloman Smith Barney Investment Firm.

Communicating a program through partnerships is not limited to the local media and newsletters. Both Partners in Education and School-to-Work programs have national offices that publicize school programs through printed newsletters and press releases, as well as through their respective Web sites. Both have updated news pages, as well as on-line newsletters or sample articles from the printed newsletters. The New York State Education Department has its own on-line School-to-Work site. School partnerships lend themselves to regional and national press. The key is in understanding the school's mission, evaluating and using your available business and community resources, and communicating the message to your target audience.

Albany High Students Get a Glimpse into Life at AMC

Program provides rewarding experience for seniors.

By Cathy Cartier Hayes

For 11 Albany High School students this has been an eye-opening year. Unlike many of their counterparts, these students arrive at "work" each morning at 8 a.m. and spend two hours in some of the most unlikely places.

The students are part of a pilot program called Health Explorations, which began in September and runs through June. The program brings the students into the Medical Center to learn about the disciplines and various departments that make up the Albany Medical Center Hospital and Albany Medical College. Monday mornings are spent in a classroom setting at the Medical Center with Chris Urbano, R.N., a teacher with the Albany City School District and coordinator of the program. During the remainder of the week, each student spends two hours every morning in one of 21 participating departments.

While some of the students, nine of whom wanted to be physicians when they arrived, have decided they are really interested in other areas of medicine, all say they have had a rewarding experience. They have had an opportunity, Urbano said, to see first hand everything from surgery and the emergency room to public relations and central supply.

Shanika Mallory, who will attend Temple this fall as a pre-med major with a minor in Spanish, said she has learned a great deal from her exposure to the different departments that make-up the Medical Center.

Some departments, Mallory said, "are not recognized in the hospital because they don't deliver patient care, like transportation and central supply, but they play a big role. They are vital to the hospital, they keep the hospital running and what they are delivering is as

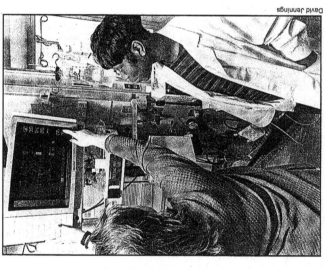

David Jennings

Joyce McCormack, R.N., B.S.N., shows Beverly Walters how a heart monitor works in the intensive care unit.

important as what a doctor is delivering."

The goal of the program, Urbano said, is to confirm that health care is the field the students want to pursue after they graduate from high school. It combines the resources of education and business and helps the students prepare to function in the adult world.

Beth Witonsky said she was originally interested in pharmacy when she began the program in September, but has now decided to pursue nursing. While doing her rotation in adult medicine, Witonsky said, she enjoyed working with the patients and being around the nurses. She now works as a nurses aide on the floor every other weekend and one

evening a week.

Mary Ellen Pavone also changed her mind about what she wants to pursue in the health field. Originally interested in biomedical research, Pavone said after spending time in physical medicine she believes that is what she would like to study. "I really like working with people," she said. During her rotation in obstetrics and gynecology, Pavone was able to witness a live birth. The experience, she said, changed her. "It's hard to explain, birth is such a miracle, seeing it in real life was incredible."

Education has been criticized for not giving high school students a sense of the work world, said Shelly Malan, R.N., nursing education director at AMC. The schools are responding to that, she believes, by beginning these types of programs which place students directly in the workplace.

The expectations are high, Isaac Hammond Jr. said, in the program. "You are expected to know certain things and that motivates you to go and ask more questions and learn more."

Jennifer Mullen, who was the only student in the program interested in being a veterinarian, was able to spend a two-week rotation at the Parkside Veterinary Hospital in Albany. She will head to the University of Massachusetts this fall to pursue a career in veterinary science.

"A lot of people have preconceived notions about what people do," Pavone said, but this program allowed her and her fellow students to have an in-depth look at what people's jobs are, how a hospital runs and how people and departments interact in providing the best care possible. "I didn't realize how important everyone – from admitting to patient care – is in making the facility run."

"The Medical Center believes in its commitment to the community," said Mary Nolan, R.N., M.S., group vice president for patient care. "This program is an opportunity to meet that commitment in a different way." ∎

Designing Newsletters and Web Sites

One major advantage of a Web site is that it allows the user to communicate with a district on their time and not necessarily when the district is open for business. It's great customer service.

—Ken Petersen, Web design coordinator,
Capital Region BOCES Communications Service

The media can be a powerful tool in conveying messages about a school's or district's mission, but they should never be the only tool. The one advantage the media have in delivery is volume. They can reach a large target audience in a short time. They may not be the most reliable tool, however. One of the most tried and true methods of disseminating information for schools has been the school newsletter. With the advent of the World Wide Web, the technology of information has changed and the newsletter has taken on a whole new meaning.

Newsletters and Web sites are available tools a school or district has for sending and receiving unfiltered information. They can provide consistent messages that can stop rumors or misinformation. Bear in mind that although a school may send a newsletter to the community or create a Web site, there is no guarantee that anyone will read it. Schools must learn and adhere to the 30-3-30 principal: Generally, readers will skim through a newspaper or newsletter at a rate of 30 seconds, 3 minutes, or 30 minutes. How well you get their attention will determine how much information is absorbed. Make your newsletter clear, concise, and understandable (see sample pages in Exhibits 7.1, 7.2, and 7.3). In other words, stay away from jargon. If you get the attention of your readers, they will want to know more and possibly become involved in a school or district.

"Newsletters and Web sites can help build awareness in the community," said Nanette Hance, Monroe One BOCES communications coordinator for the Rush-Henrietta Central School District in Rochester, New York. "As a communications vehicle, they help bring recognition to a school or district. You can talk about the things you can't elsewhere."

WASHOE COUNTY SCHOOL DISTRICT

PARENTS

Volume V, Issue 1

School Bond Issue Headed For November Ballot

Following months of work and dozens of meetings, the legal hurdles have all been cleared for the district's bond issue to appear on the general election ballot November 3. The two-part question is designed to address the district's most critical need for three new high schools and also give voters the ability to decide on funding for four elementary schools and an alternative/technical school. In addition, the ballot questions will allow voters to decide on whether to approve $15 million for upgrading and reconstructing existing schools.

This unique two-part question responds to input from more than 40 community meetings and a community-wide public opinion poll. Public sentiment solidly agreed with the immediate need to solve high school overcrowding, but many citizens appearing at the

"Yes, Yes for Kids."
The bond campaign official kick-off was July 13.

public meetings wanted the district to take a longer outlook and address the need for more elementary schools called for in the district's Long Range Facility Plan. An overwhelming 92 percent in the opinion poll supported upgrading and improving existing schools.

Part A of the bond issue, totaling about $131 million, contains three new high schools, one in Spanish Springs, one in the North Valley and the third in the southeast. The two schools in the north will be designed to accommodate 1,800 students. The southeast school's opening capacity will be 1,500. All three can be expanded later to 2,000 students. Part A also contains $6 million for upgrades and improvements at existing schools.

Part A would not increase the tax rate above its current level because existing bonds are being retired, the new bonds would be sold in stages and the county's assessed valuation is increasing.

Part B of the bond issue, totaling about $47 million, would fund three new elementary schools in the Truckee Meadows and a new satellite elementary school in Incline Village. Even with the move to multi-track, year-round schedules, these schools are needed between now and the year 2004. Part B also has funds for a technical/alternative school and another $9 million for upgrading existing schools. If Part B is approved, the owner of a $150,000 new home would see a tax increase of approximately $21 a year. The tax rate would increase 4 cents per $100 of assessed valuation.

The bonds in Part B would be issued only if both Part B and Part A pass. Voters will be able to vote for either or both parts of the question.

For the first time, this bond issue sets aside funds for extraordinary maintenance of the new facilities. About $650,000 in Part A and $235,000 in Part B is earmarked for such uses.

The school district's proposal was unanimously approved by the county's Debt Management Commission on May 29. This commission is charged with ensuring that the proposal meets a "public need" and does not, if passed, exceed the state's property tax cap. The measure also received the endorsement of the School Facilities Oversight Panel, established in each county by the last Legislature in AB 353. This committee is made up of representatives from each of the local governments and the general public.

More information on the bond issue is available by calling the **Communications Office at 348-0371.**

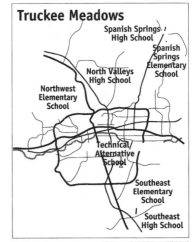

Truckee Meadows

Spanish Springs High School
Spanish Springs Elementary School
North Valleys High School
Northwest Elementary School
Technical/Alternative School
Southeast Elementary School
Southeast High School

Incline Village

◯ = Existing Schools,
Elementary, Middle
and High

Satellite Elementary School

Lake Tahoe

EXHIBIT 7.2. Washoe County School District *PARENTS* Newsletter, Page 5
SOURCE: Washoe County School District; used by permission.

What Did YOU Do Over Summer Break?

We know what more than a thousand students did during their summer break – they participated in the first WCSD Summer School Literacy Project. Students going into the fourth and fifth grades, as well as students entering the eighth and ninth grades, were recommended to attend summer school this year as an opportunity to focus on building their literacy and math skills. Literacy Centers were created in 19 elementary schools and in two middle schools.

In an effort to make this a productive and positive experience for students, the Read & Succeed program was developed. The main objective of Read & Succeed is to match the resources of the district and community with the students who need extra help with literacy skills. Community resources include: recruiting Read & Succeed volunteers, working volunteers and providing incentives for students as they meet reading goals.

KTVN Channel 2 was a tremendous help in getting the word about becoming a Read & Succeed volunteer. Additionally, three KTVN employees became Read & Succeed volunteers. The Reno Chukars invited all the third- and fourth-grade Literacy Centers to participate in their Frequent Readers incentive program. Students read fervently in order to earn Chukars' goodies, such as T-shirts, hats, autographed baseballs and tickets to games. And, like KTVN, players from the Chukars volunteered their time to be guest readers in Literacy Centers. Be assured, "Casey at the Bat" takes on added meaning when read by a professional athlete.

All in all, more than 60 individuals answered our call to spend some of their summertime with students. Volunteers reflected a variety of backgrounds and perspectives, including high school and college students, parents, individuals from the business world and the faith community, service/professional organizations such as the Reno Lions Club and the Northern Nevada Chapter of the AAUW and WCSD employees. All Read & Succeed volunteers had two important things in common, an enjoyment of reading and a desire to help children succeed in school and life. Whether volunteers read aloud to students and/or listened to students read, they worked under the direction of teachers to provide much needed individual attention and encouragement to students.

So, what did you do this summer? Many can answer: "I was a Read & Succeed volunteer. I helped kids become better readers."

Esther Bennett Elementary School Opens

Esther Bennett Elementary School is the last major school district facility built using 1992 Bond Issue money. It is 56,481-square-feet and was designed for 600-plus students with 12 standard classrooms of about 900 square feet each, 12 "class-size reduction" classrooms of about 750 square feet each, a Library with the potential use as a partnership library (for public and school use) at a later date, four special education rooms, Computer Room, Music Room, Teacher's Lounge and work areas and an "interior court" for multi-use space (cafeteria and theater).

Construction began November 3, 1997, and the doors open for the first day of school on Monday, August 31. Dianne Longson will serve as Bennett's first principal.

You Should Be Committed... Committed To Kids!

Join us at the Fifth Annual Committed to Kids Celebration

11 a.m. to 2 p.m. Saturday, September 26 Meadowood Mall

KTVN Channel 2, Barker Business Systems and Meadowood Mall have teamed up to provide a fun-filled day dedicated to honoring and celebrating the thousands of volunteers who show their commitment to the students in our schools. School volunteers and volunteers active in Partners in Education programs will receive special recognition and a gift of appreciation. Mark your calendar so you won't miss out on a day of entertainment, volunteer information and great shopping discounts. Together, we make a difference for kids!

5

Both newsletters and Web sites can be viewed as tools used in fulfilling district or school goals. Again, a school administrator should review the school's or district's goals and determine how those messages need to be incorporated into a communications plan. "Many people don't have access to the Web," said Hance. "That's why it's a good idea to blend both tools in a school's communications plan."

"We try to talk about educational initiatives in the district, the things that might be issues, as well as board and budget information. It's also a recognition tool for students and teachers," said Hance. "But schools need to remember that they are competing to capture the attention of every other person in the community. The message should be consistent. Districts don't always understand that. There needs to be continuity and clarity."

According to Hance, one area of difficulty in the Rush-Henrietta Central School District was that every school was sending home newsletters. "People have less and less time to read," she said. "If you have three kids and three different newsletters, where's the consistency? We dealt with it by having a district page in each of the school's newsletters so that the same district information was being conveyed" (see Exhibit 7.8).

Much of the content and use of newsletters was described in Chapter 2, "Building Credibility and Accountability With the Community," but schools and districts should consider some additional guidelines before creating a newsletter or Web site.

In creating a newsletter, educators should ask the following questions:

- *What is the content? What's news?* You need to discuss the good and the bad. Keep a newsletter in news-style format—most important information first, then filler, or "feel good" news.

- *Who is the target audience? To whom are you writing? What do they want to know?*

- *What's the budget? Can you create/print a newsletter in-house, or do you need to hire a freelance designer/ writer? What's the circulation?* The number of people you are trying to reach will determine the cost of printing and postage.

- *How will it be disseminated? Will you mail it or send it home with students?*

- *Is the material newsworthy (is it something you would want to read)? Does it answer the important questions the community needs to know?*

Schools are limited by money, so in creating a newsletter, first look to your available resources. Does anyone on staff have a background in computer graphics? Do you have in-house printing capabilities? Do you have a bulk mail permit with the post office to send material at a reduced rate?

Many schools adopt a laissez-faire attitude toward communications. Everyone (e.g., board members, administrators, school personnel, teachers, parents) stresses the importance of it but doesn't always grasp the process. Communications involves a commitment of time and resources (human and financial). As much thought should be placed on what a school or district's message is as is placed on curriculum. One is not more important than the other. Communications is *not* a fringe benefit.

First, develop a mechanism for finding newsworthy events. Many school districts have news or event tip sheets available in each building (see examples in Exhibits 7.4, 7.5, and 7.6). Tip sheets help with developing story ideas. The sheets should have all the basic information, such as *who, what, when, where, and how,* and the name and telephone number of the lead contact person. As events come up, the tip sheets are then forwarded to a school or district communications liaison. Tip sheets can help the communications liaison determine whether an event is directed primarily at a district audience or merits media attention.

(Text continues on page 103)

EXHIBIT 7.3. *Team Springfield* Newsletter, Front Page
SOURCE: Springfield (Oregon) Public Schools; used by permission.

TEAM Springfield

A COMMUNITY NEWSLETTER PUBLISHED BY WILLAMALANE, THE CITY OF SPRINGFIELD, AND SPRINGFIELD PUBLIC SCHOOLS

ONE DAY IN SPRINGFIELD SCHOOL DISTRICT #19...
Did You Know?

Springfield School District #19 is the fifth largest employer in Lane County. Each month, 1200 people receive a paycheck from Springfield School District #19. Only the U of O, Lane County government, City of Eugene and Eugene School District employ more people than

The students arrive at 16 elementary schools, five middle schools, two high schools and Gateways Learning Center (an alternative program for middle and high-school age youth).

One thousand, two hundred six students eat breakfast at school before going to class. In class — 606 teachers greet the

students receive all those subjects plus fine and applied arts. High school students also choose from electives in foreign language, vocational education, government, global education, personal finance and career development.

Other requirements include: age-appropriate plans of

WHY ARE YOU GETTING THIS NEWSLETTER?

Last year, we learned from a survey of Springfield voters that more than half of you feel you don't have enough information to make thoughtful decisions about Springfield's future.

So, the city and the school and park districts are teaming up to provide more information on a regular basis. If you live within Springfield's urban growth boundary, or School District #19's or Willamalane's district boundaries, you'll be receiving Team Springfield about three times a year.

We hope it'll be information you can use. And we welcome your feedback—good or bad! There's a comment form you can clip out and mail back to let us know what you'd like more information about.

And thanks for taking a few minutes to read Team Springfield.

secretaries work at the schools. | middle school kids stay after

EXHIBIT 7.3. Continued

...City of Eugene and Eugene School District employ more people than Springfield School District #19.

The district covers an area of over 187 square miles stretching as far south as Goshen and as far north as the McKenzie River, the Mohawk valley to near Marcola and the Camp Creek valley. The boundary travels east past Leaburg to a point near the Vida Lea Trailer Courts on Highway 126.

As 11,278 students wake up to get ready for school each weekday, 70 bus drivers transport 5,249 students 2,060 miles to school. Six thousand students walk or receive rides to school.

...six students eat breakfast at school before going to class. In class — 606 teachers greet the students — but they won't all recognize each other. On an average day students will be met by 35 substitute teachers and 13 new students.

Elementary students receive instruction in the areas of reading, writing, language arts, math and music. Middle school

...education, personal fitness and career development.

Other requirements include: age-appropriate plans of instruction regarding infectious diseases, including HIV and Hepatitis B, drug and alcohol abuse prevention and sex education; Women's History Week; History of Oregon Statehood; Arbor Week; emergency drills; gang prevention; community service and instruction in ethics. A portion of school days must also be set aside for observation and instruction regarding Lincoln's Birthday, Oregon's Birthday, Washington's Birthday, Columbus Day, Martin Luther King Day and President's Day.

Three hundred forty-two support staff, teacher aides, and secretaries work at the schools. Sixty-six cooks serve 4,916 hot lunches; 2,200 at free or reduced price.

One thousand five hundred seventy-nine students receive special services for speech and language, reading, math, behavior problems, physical therapy, autism or other special needs.

Thirty-three principals and assistant principals suspend 9-10 students for misbehavior during a school day. The majority of the suspensions are for defiance of teachers, but some are for fighting, disruption of class or obscene language. Once per week, the district will expel a student for serious misbehavior.

At the end of the school day 70 bus drivers pick up 5,249 students at school and drive 2,060 miles to take them home. Each day, district buses have 4,120 miles added to their odometers.

However, the day doesn't end for the school district. In fact, the district buildings will continue to be used for another 278 hours each day.

Four hundred ninety-nine middle school kids stay after school to participate in 33 different activities and 151 high school students stay after school to participate in 15 student clubs. Ninety-nine high school students stay after school to compete on athletic teams. There are 30 hours of practice and four athletic events each night.

Approximately 80% of the after-hours activity is actually coordinated by community groups such as Kidsports, Willamalane and AYSO. As these various groups use the buildings and grounds, 57 custodians are quietly at work - cleaning 1,691,524 square feet of buildings for the next morning.

Springfield Welcomes Glenwood

In December, Lane County and the cities of Eugene and Springfield agreed to transfer jurisdiction of Glenwood from Eugene to Springfield. In February the Lane County Local Government Boundary Commission approved a request to transfer the industrial area in west Glenwood from Eugene to Springfield.

What do these changes mean? The industrial area will receive full city services from Springfield. Residents in unincorporated Glenwood will continue to be part of the County, but will come to Springfield with planning and building requests. Residents will continue to receive fire and emergency medical help from Springfield and have access to the facilities of Willamalane Park and Recreation District. For more information, contact Mark Metzger, 726-3753.

Team Springfield

EXHIBIT 7.4. City School District of Albany *News Tip . . .* Sheet
SOURCE: City School District of Albany; used by permission.

News Tip...

City School District of Albany
Office of Public Information

*I*s something newsworthy happening in your school? Then let us know.

Newsworthy items include upcoming events, honors or achievements, part-nerships, grant funding, programs, creative use of resources -- in short, any-thing significant or unusual that the public might not know about but would find interesting.

Please provide some information about your news item.

Who? _____
_____

What? _____
_____
_____

When? _____
_____

Where? _____
_____

Why? _____
_____

How? _____
_____
_____

Describe any photo opportunities or visuals that will exist at the event. _____
_____
_____

List the name and phone number of the contact person for this item. _____

Also list your name and phone number (if different from above).
_____

Date submitted _____ School _____

EXHIBIT 7.5. City School District of Albany *News Recap . . .* Sheet
SOURCE: City School District of Albany; used by permission.

News Recap...

Anything interesting happen last month? Let us know as well.

Please describe any newsworthy items that occurred in your school last month?

____
____
____
____
____
____
____

Please describe any publicity generated by the event?

____
____
____
____

Thank you for your cooperation.

Information provided on the "News Tips" form will be used to develop story concepts for local and state media, school district publications, and to keep administrators and board members informed about activities in the schools. Call the public information department at 462-7228 with any questions.

Please return this form to:

Department of Communications
City School District of Albany
Academy Park
Albany, NY 12207

FAX TO 3 5 3 - 5 5 3 6

DATE:

SCHOOL:

SCHOOL CONTACT:

SCHOOL PHONE:

PARTNER:

PARTNER CONTACT:

PARTNER PHONE:

DESCRIPTION OF EVENT OR ANNOUNCEMENT:

_____

_____

_____

_____

_____

_____

_____

_____

_____

_____

_____

_____

_____

_____

For Example: A group of teachers received a grant to participate in a workshop on raising educational standards. Their goal is to bring back to the district the tools necessary to implement change. Although it's an important piece of information, what communications tool would be most appropriate? The most likely tool would be the newsletter or a staff newsletter, although the school could certainly issue a press release. As stated earlier, the media are not predictable, and they could do a story on it, but the newsletter would reach your target audience—parents and taxpayers.

Second, once you know what you want to say, how are you going to say it? At this point, conferring with a knowledgeable communications person or graphic designer can help. Many computer software programs include templates a school can use as a shell in building a newsletter. Because the school is conveying a message to its shareholders, however, how a newsletter looks is nearly as important as content. You want people to pick it up and read it. Graphic design can add a whole layer of concept to your message, apart from the written word. Design adds a feeling.

If money is available, consult with a graphic designer in shaping the look of the newsletter. Designers can create a template, or shell, that a school liaison can use each time a newsletter is created, merely by dropping new copy into it. It is a good investment in something that could conceivably have a long shelf life. A school or district logo, as well as its theme or mission statement, can be blended into the cover page of a newsletter.

A designer can help you determine the size of the newsletter, as well as suggest color schemes. Much of the look will be governed by budget. More money equals more color, higher quality paper stock, and a larger circulation. Schools may be limited to printing in-house, which often restricts newsletter format and the amount of ink used.

Third, determine who is going to receive the newsletter and how it will be distributed. Can you trust that if you send something home with students it will reach parents and guardians? In elementary school, that is highly probable, but in middle and high schools, the probability drops sharply.

In 1989, when the City School District of Albany began publishing its first newsletter, *Capital Education*, it was distributed to every homeowner within the city's limits, or approximately 40,000 residents. The goal was to reach all taxpayers, and not just parents. Within a few years, the volume of recipients became cost prohibitive. The original three-color glossy publication retained its basic graphic look, but it was replaced with a matte stock paper and only two colors. Eventually, the number of recipients was reduced only to student households, or approximately 10,000 residents. This tactic saved money, but did all the district's shareholders receive needed information?

Newsletter distribution can become a balancing act between fiscal responsibility and the public's right to know. Like any other business, schools should market their newsletters at special events, such as school concerts, parent-teacher nights, plays, and athletic events. A school can distribute newsletters as part of an overall marketing/informational package when potential parents call requesting information on the school.

Basic Dos and Don'ts of Newsletters

- Keep to a news-style format; write in the third person; avoid using *we.*

- Place more important articles first—then, fill in with "feel good" stories. Write about the issues people are discussing or want to hear about.

- Keep articles short and to the point.

- Include important school/district information where possible, such as telephone numbers, names, upcoming events, and meetings.

- Use quotes, photographs, and humor to break up the text. Stay away from "talking head" shots of administrators. Readers will be more interested in students and fun activities.

- Be first with school/district news (good or bad).

- Use two or three columns in the layout, and use a ragged right, rather than justified column.

- Use "pull out" quotes to emphasize a point; it grabs the reader's attention.

- Check and recheck information for accuracy. When quoting someone's opinion, be sure to include facts backing up the information.

- Be timely.

- Avoid jargon.

- Stay away from newsletters longer than 4 to 6 pages—you'll lose readers.

- Stay away from using too many fonts and those that are hard to read.

Web Sites

Ken Petersen is the Web design coordinator for the Capital Region BOCES Communications Service in Albany, New York. One of a handful of different services offered to schools, Web design is a relatively new, yet highly sought-after service.

"When we first launched the Mohonasen Web site, I heard from skeptics who said, 'Yeah, but how many people in our community are actually on-line?' Well, that was almost 4 years ago, and I can tell you there are a lot more people on-line now than when we started. We're a lot further along with our site because we did jump in early," said Deborah Bush-Suflita, BOCES public information specialist to the Rotterdam Mohonasen Central School District.

Bush-Suflita, who also writes and edits the district's newsletter, has become the Webmaster as well. With the advent of the Internet, her role as a communications professional has changed in recent years. "The number of people on-line is growing at staggering rates. You would be hard-pressed to find someone who hasn't heard of the World Wide Web today," she said. "Yet, the Web didn't even exist when Bill Clinton was first inaugurated. I tell people who are skeptical about investing in Web communications that it is only a matter of time before computers and Internet connections are as common as televisions, VCRs, and telephones in American homes. It is fast becoming *the* way to get information and do business in our society. Schools cannot afford to ignore this fact. Web sites play a major role in providing information to individuals seeking information about school districts before moving to a new geographic location," added Hance, "Especially those who are technology proficient."

When school districts contact BOCES for Web site development, Petersen says, he has a 9-step process that helps schools and districts get on-line quickly and efficiently. "We first ask the school or district to assemble a steering committee composed of a technology person, a communications specialist if they have one, teachers, administrators, and a graphic designer," he said. "Then, we ask, 'What's the purpose? What do you want a site to do?' "

Step 1: Organize a steering committee.

Step 2: Determine the purpose for the Web site. What's the target audience? What's your budget, and how interactive do you want your site to be?

Step 3: Meet with the Web site designer and begin the conceptual process.

Step 4: Develop blueprint/sketches for the Web site. The steering committee meets and approves/makes changes.

Step 5: Develop the Web site on-screen. This step is collaboration between the graphic designer and the Web designer.

Step 6: Once the site is constructed, the committee reviews it and decides who will provide content. What should go on it? Where should it go? Who will be responsible for updating and approving all content?

Step 7: Once the site is on-screen and the content is provided, the committee should make sure it is working properly and make any necessary changes before it is uploaded to the server.

Step 8: Determine who will host the site—in-house? regional information center? or local Internet service provider?

Step 9: Review the site in 6 months to determine its effectiveness.

Many schools and districts want information the community can view but are often uncertain about content. Although Web site development is in its adolescent stages for many schools, it is not unlike determining content for newsletters. Web sites, however, can add material that would be too lengthy for newsletters, such as an alumni base for distributing class reunion information.

In fact, Hance said, "It's critical that there is coordination and continuity between Web sites and other published district information." One should promote the other. It does little good to have a Web site if no one knows it exists. All printed materials, including business cards and letterheads, should not only include telephone and fax numbers, but the Web site address as well.

"When you talk about trying to improve communication between home and school, you can't ignore the Web," said Bush-Suflita. "It's a terrific tool with immense potential for linking parents and teachers. Unlike print publications, the Web is immediate and allows for two-way communication. I get all kinds of feedback through Mohonasen's Web site that lets us know what's on people's minds. Some days it's taxes, some days it's school safety, and some days it's simple questions like, 'What's the date for kindergarten orientation?' "

According to Bush-Suflita, the Mohonasen district encourages visitors to the site to respond to what they see by dashing off a quick e-mail. "They are more than happy to take those few minutes to tell me what they think the district is doing right and what they think it's doing wrong. You simply can't get that kind of immediate feedback from a print publication."

Ken Petersen said that schools must think in terms of customer service, much like any business. How responsive or responsible a school wants to be to its constituents will determine content. The first part is design and implementation; the second and more important part is maintenance.

"Highly interactive sites have hyperlinks, forms to fill out, and surveys. It allows a teacher or student or parent to communicate with the school via the Web," said Petersen. "But you need someone to constantly update, add, and delete information. If you don't, it becomes like a course guide, where it's outdated very quickly."

Bush-Suflita adds that today's younger parents are more computer savvy. "Today's college students cut their teeth on this technology and are incredibly Web savvy. They expect to be able to find useful information on-line, and when they can't find it, they'll be sure to let you know!" she said. "This generation is fast becoming the parents of today's kindergartners. Schools that want to keep a customer focus cannot afford to overlook the Web. It's quick and effective."

When looking to create a school/district Web site (see sample Web pages in Exhibits 7.7 through 7.13), Petersen suggests, first look to your local school support services network. If no Web design services are available, then contact your local Internet service provider. Many local Internet companies have Web designers on staff. What you want the Web site to do will determine the cost and scope of the project. The more interactive the site, the greater the amount of programming and the higher the cost. "The biggest cost to a district is manpower to keep it up to date," said Petersen. "Programming, layout, and navigational items all play a factor. I'd first ask the company if they have done any other sites for schools," said Petersen.

Petersen also suggests that school Web sites use a statistical package that keeps track of activity on the site. A statistical package can track how many "hits," or visits, that site has received, which pages are being accessed, what time of day the site is most active, where the visitors are coming from to find the site, and how much time is spent on each page. As a result, the school/district can then determine what pieces of information are the most relevant—whether it's basketball scores, lunch menus, bus routes, or the on-line newsletter. The Web-hosting service usually provides these statistical packages. "That way, if a school is looking to have one page more prominent than other, they'll know that lunch menus are getting more hits than, let's say, bus routes," said Petersen. "Keep lunch menus up front. It's all about customer service."

And, good communication.

EXHIBIT 7.7. Rush-Henrietta Central School District Web Site Home Page
SOURCE: Rush-Henrietta Central School District; used by permission.

Explore Rush-Henrietta Central School District

Site Index
Site Search

Visitor Center
Staff
Parents
Current Events
School Index
Student Center
Bulletin Board Service

Our Electronic Bulletin Board may share your information with us! Please send any information you would like to share to our postmaster. Our postmaster will place your mail into the most appropriate place on our BBS.

Questions or concerns about this server contact the friendly Webmaster

(c) 1998 Rush-Henrietta Central School District

Welcome Visitors! - Learn through the following pages all about our District and please sign our guest book.

District Overview

School Index

District Map

Community Opportunities

Please sign our Guest Book

Input to or Search the Alumni database

Staff Center

From the Board of Education

March 1999

Dear Residents:

The Board of Education is currently working on two very important district issues, the 1999-2000 school budget and space needs among all our schools.

The annual budget process affects every stakeholder in our school community. The final budget will be a blueprint of our priorities. The budget process starts in August, heats up from November through April, and culminates with the district vote on May 18, 1999, the statewide school voting day.

Unlike other government budgets affecting our community, every registered voter has the opportunity to vote on our school district's budget. Recognizing this, the Board of Education over the past few years has made the budget process very open. Anyone from the community is welcome to join or attend the Budget Advisory Committee, which meets from late fall to early spring. Any Board member or the Superintendent is available to receive comments and suggestions. In fact, the present budget process is meant to foster communication and discussion as we reexamine our priorities, evaluate our resources and plan the most effective ways we can achieve these priorities.

A brochure giving details on the final budget adopted by the Board will be mailed to all residences in the school district in May. For more information about the Rush-Henrietta budget process at this time, please see the article in this newsletter or contact any school board member.

As this newsletter went to press, the Board was still discussing options for future use of space. Dr. McKanna, Superintendent of Schools, has made the following recommendations:

• Begin the movement of special education students from the Vollmer School into the five current K-5 schools until all Vollmer students are integrated.

• Redistrict students living in University of Rochester graduate student housing so they would attend Winslow Elementary rather than Fyle Elementary School, in order to reduce the out-of-proportion enrollment at Fyle.

• Don't change the middle school boundary lines, except that students from the University of Rochester graduate student housing would go to Roth along with the other Winslow students.

• Accommodate increasing enrollment at the Senior High School by moving ninth grade students to the Webster Building in year 2000-2001.

The Board of Education welcomes your insights into the education provided by the Rush-Henrietta Central School District. You may contact any of us directly and are most welcome to attend Board of Education meetings.

Sincerely,
A. Dirk Hightower, *President*

Teachers Are the Prizes

A unique fund-raising effort was sponsored by the Burger Middle School Spanish Club and Community Service Club. Students bought chances to spend part of a day with their favorite staff members. Thirty staff members agreed to be the prizes! A total of $218 was raised, and all proceeds were donated to the American Red Cross Hurricane Relief Efforts in Central America. Lisa Palmieri won 6th grade science teacher Lisa Craig.

Initiatives Help Raise Standards

Many initiatives in the Rush-Henrietta Central School District are meant to raise standards that support higher student achievement. These are just a few examples.

• **The PM Study Center** at the Senior High School offers help in all subjects. Every Monday through Thursday from 3:00-3:45 p.m., students can go to the study center in the library to find a quiet place to study, a wealth of learning resources and friendly teachers eager to help. Teachers with expertise in English and social studies are available on Mondays and Tuesdays, and teachers with expertise in science and math are available Wednesdays and Thursdays.

• A pilot **Middle School Academic Policy** went into effect March 1 to "raise the bar" for students who may sacrifice their studies for extracurricular activities. Students passing all school subjects are eligible to participate. Students failing one or more subjects during a five week interim are required to attend an after-school homework program before attending activities. Students failing three or more subjects are ineligible to participate in activities during the five week interim period.

• **Homework Guidelines** for elementary students and secondary students have been developed for consistency in the amount of homework assigned, the conditions on which homework is graded and the percent that homework contributes to a student's grade. These guidelines have been incorporated into booklets and distributed to parents so they will understand what is expected of their children and can help them meet these expectations.

• **First Steps** is a resource used districtwide for observing the writing and reading development of students from kindergarten through grade eight. These observations allow teachers to see where students are on a developmental continuum. First Steps has instructional strategies for both teachers and parents to help improve student achievement.

2

EXHIBIT 7.9. Rush-Henrietta Central School District Web Site Student View Page
SOURCE: Rush-Henrietta Central School District; used by permission.

Student View

Leadership, Learning & Life

by Diana Richter

"Shake your foot! Shake, shake, shake, shake your foot!" a crowd of nearly 400 students and their advisors whispered, then repeated three more times, with the fourth reaching almost spastic proportions, "Shake your foot!

Shake, shake, shake, shake your foot!!" And there were corybantic movements too, of course. A stranger, with good reason, would be taken aback observing such a scene. But at the New York State Advisor Student Association leadership conference, what else could be expected?

On March 9, 30 enthusiastic, open-minded Rush-Henrietta Senior High School students attended the fourth annual conference at the Nazareth College Arts Center. They were psyched to have a good time and, indeed, they did. Twenty-one high schools, from Penn Yan to Aquinas, gathered to share ideas about "Building School Unity Through Leadership." To get things started and to make new friends, students engaged in "fringing," the activity in which a person gives a peer a hearty greeting, introduces his or herself, and ties a string around the new companion's yarn necklace, following-up with a hug. An easy way to break the ice, fringing eliminates the barriers that often form with school rivalries.

The day was spent participating in workshops. Among the presenters, were R-H's Student Council officers. Mike Daniels (treasurer), Lindsey Hettis (recording secretary), and Sarah Fischette (corresponding secretary) offered a workshop, "A+ For the Teacher/Faculty Appreciation," while Shamir Rhodes (vice president) and Kristen Mancari (president) gave a workshop called "Chicken Soup for the Leadership Soul." Various other sessions addressed issues including diversity awareness, school spirit, student recognition, and advisor concerns.

Culminating in a final idea exchange, the student leaders learned of activities and events that have been successful elsewhere in promoting a unified school front. The highlight of the day was keynote speaker Patrick George, a "vertically-challenged brown man," as he referred to himself. His energy was contagious; everyone was totally engrossed in his stories and accounts of overcoming adversity, taking the steps necessary to reach one's goals, and not letting "dream assassins" interfere. His willingness to share personal experiences invoked both tears and smiles among audience members. His messages were strong.

As the Rush-Henrietta delegates exited the halls of Nazareth, the boys robustly chanted, "Go! Go-go! Go mighty R-H! Go! Go-go!" The girls simultaneously chimed "Go-o-o-o! Migh-ty R-H!" It was evident that the students were bringing back a profound energy to their school.

Diana Richter is a junior at R-H Senior High School.

New State Tests Begin this Year

As of this year, students across New York are required to take more challenging state tests in school. Fourth graders in Rush-Henrietta elementary schools, along with other 4th graders throughout the state, began the more rigorous testing as they took the state's new three-day English exam in January. The test was an initial step in the drive toward higher standards statewide and part of a testing system intended to help ensure that students are acquiring the skills needed to succeed.

The 4th grade English Language Arts Assessment was the first step toward raising standards beginning with the early grades. The format of the new test is different from the Reading PEP formerly given at the end of third grade. It involved reading and listening to short passages and answering multiple-choice and other questions about the passages. Students also were expected to write short compositions.

Students in Ann Looby's 4th grade class at Fyle Elementary School were interviewed about the test for the "Young Views" column of the *Democrat & Chronicle*. Briana Meacham said, "The test made me feel like I was in college. It was fair because we did not have a lot to do. They could make it easier, though. I think that's my suggestion: Change the test by making it a little easier."

The tests were evaluated at regional scoring centers on three days. Teachers did not grade papers belonging to their own classes. Test results are expected in May.

According to Dr. Helena Spring, Assistant Superintendent for Instruction, the assessment results will offer an opportunity for the District to see where strengths in both teaching and learning lie. "Results will also help to identify areas in our educational program that need improvement in order to raise academic achievement levels. They will show whether students are meeting the higher academic standards now required and if they are on track to passing the Regents exam required in high school," said Dr. Spring.

"Today there is an intense focus on what a student is actually learning. Students are now being evaluated for problem-solving and critical thinking skills, rather than just having to answer multiple-choice and true/false questions," Dr. Spring said.

This June, 4th graders will begin taking the state's new math test. It will include multiple-choice and short-answer questions that focus on arithmetic, measurement and mathematical reasoning. New science tests for 4th graders will begin in the spring of 2000 and will also include multiple-choice questions and questions that require short answers, as well as a laboratory project.

> *For more information regarding the tougher state tests and how they will impact all students, contact Dr. Helena Spring, Assistant Superintendent for Instruction, at 359-5015.*

6

EXHIBIT 7.10. Washoe County School District Web Site Home Page
SOURCE: Washoe County School District; used by permission.

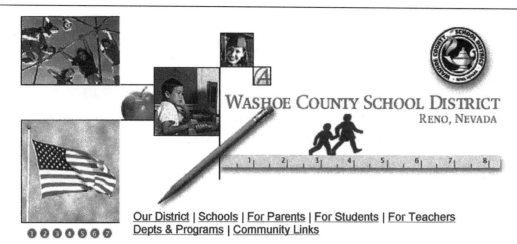

WELCOME

Welcome to the Washoe County School District, Nevada's second largest district. Serving the Reno/Sparks and Lake Tahoe region, WCSD enrolls nearly 53,000 students in 83 schools, employs almost 6,000 teachers, counselors, administrators and support personnel, and covers all of Washoe County.

This site has been designed as a one-stop shopping center for information about our programs, our people and our services. If you cannot find what you are looking for, please call our Communications Office at **775-348-0371** or e-mail the Director of Communications, Dr. Steve Mulvenon at **smulvenon@washoe.k12.nv.us.**

Our District | Schools | For Parents | For Students | For Teachers
Depts & Programs | Community Links

Website designed and hosted by Aztech Cyberspace, Inc

http://wcsd.aztech-cs.com/ 5/31/99

EXHIBIT 7.11. Washoe County School District Web Site Breaking News Page
SOURCE: Washoe County School District; used by permission.

WASHOE COUNTY SCHOOL DISTRICT
RENO, NEVADA

Our District | Schools | For Parents | For Students | For Teachers
Depts & Programs | Community Links | Main

BREAKING NEWS

May 28, 1999	**NEW HIGH SCHOOL SITE ALTERNATIVES CONTINUE TO BE EXPLORED**
May 28, 1999	**TWENTY NAMES TO GO TO SCHOOL BOARD FOR NEW SCHOOLS**
May 28, 1999	**SUSPICIOUS PACKAGE AT MCQUEEN HS NOT A BOMB, REWARD OFFERED BY SECRET WITNESS**
May 28, 1999	**SUSPICIOUS PACKAGE EVACUATES, CLOSES MCQUEEN HIGH SCHOOL**
May 25, 1999	**A,B,C'S BRIEFS: TEACHER RETIREMENTS, SMITH SCHOLARSHIPS & WAL-MART TEACHER OF THE YEAR**
May 25, 1999	**A,B,C'S BRIEFS: LITERACY AWARD HONOREES, SILVER STAR AWARD WINNERS & STUDENT ART WINS NATIONAL EXHIBIT**
May 25, 1999	**SCHOOL DISTRICT ALERTS PUBLIC OF OLD FILE DESTRUCTION**
May 21, 1999	**STUDENT SPACE STILL AVAILABLE AT TMCC HS FOR NEXT SCHOOL YEAR**
May 21, 1999	**TCI CABLE SPONSORS ANDERSON ES STUDENTS FOR JOB SHADOWING PROGRAM -- NEXT TOUR MAY 25!**
May 21, 1999	**GET TEED OFF AT GOLF TOURNAMENT BENEFITTING SUN VALLEY TEEN CENTER**

Our District

- Our Superintendent
- Our Board
- Fast Facts
- FAQ's
- Breaking News
- Events Calendar
- Policies & Regulations
- Website Guidelines

Breaking News

http://wcsd.aztech-cs.com/district/press_releases/   5/31/99

EXHIBIT 7.12. Rotterdam Mohonasen Web Site Home Page

SOURCE: Reprinted with permission of Deborah Bush-Suflita, communications coordinator for the Mohonasen Central School District. Graphic design by Denise LaRocque, BOCES Communications Service.

Last Updated 5.28.99

LINKS

Budget Passes 1040 to 625|

New Safe Schools Plan |

Fast FAQs |

Visit Our Schools |

Construction Project Update
|

Calendar On Line |

Report Cards On Line |

Newsletters On Line |

GRADES 9-12
MOHONASEN
HIGH SCHOOL

GRADES 6-8
DRAPER
MIDDLE SCHOOL

GRADES 3-5
PINEWOOD
INTERMEDIATE SCHOOL

GRADES K-2
BRADT
PRIMARY SCHOOL

 What's New?: Check this page out weekly for the latest news about our schools, upcoming events, Board of Education actions and our "cool web picks" of the month.

 Fast FAQs: Answers to common questions about district enrollment, the annual budget, our community and more.

 Visit our Schools: 10 things to check out at each of Mohonasen's four schools. Exciting stuff!

 Construction Project Update: Follow the progress of Mohonasen's $20 million building project.

 Calendar on Line: Our web calendar is updated frequently so check here for the latest information on scheduled events (including changes and additions from our print calendar!)

Report Cards on Line: The on-line version of Mohonasen's annual report on student test scores. Where we're strong, where we need to improve and what we're doing to get there.

 Newsletters On-line: The printed newsletters that Mohonasen mails to residents

http://www.mohonasen.org/   5/31/99

EXHIBIT 7.13. Rotterdam Mohonasen Web Site What's New Page

SOURCE: Reprinted with permission of Deborah Bush-Suflita, communications coordinator for the Mohonasen Central School District. Graphic design by Denise LaRocque, BOCES Communications Service.

Last Updated: 5.28.99

| In the News | Board of Education | School Events & Meetings | Cool Web Picks | New on our School Pages |

In the News

Budget passes by decisive margin

School WILL be in session on May 28

Pinewood Student Council award

Summer Enrichment

Construction alters summer schedules

Mohonasen has new Safe Schools Plan

Mohonasen budget passes by decisive margin

delPrado, French and Severino elected to the Board

On May 18, voters approved the 1999-2000 school budget by a margin of 1040 "yes" votes to 625 "no" votes.

The $28.9 million spending plan carries an estimated tax hike of about 3.52%. For the average Rotterdam homeowner with a house assessed at $4,000, next year's estimated tax increase will be $46.36 -- or about $3.86 more per month, before STAR exemptions.

In Guilderland and Colonie (where houses are assessed at full value), residents would pay about $0.57 and $0.55 more, respectively, per thousand dollars of assessment.

Voters also approved a proposition to purchase four buses and one van by a vote of 1140 to 490.

Three elected to school board

Also on May 18, voters elected three candidates to serve on Mohonasen's seven member Board of Education: Nancy del Prado with 883 votes, Eileen French with 711 votes and Pete Severino with 688 votes. Both del Prado and French were elected to three year terms beginning July 1. Severino, the third highest vote-getter, was elected to a one year term beginning June 7. (Severino will fill out the remainder of James Male's elected term which was temporarily filled by John Gahan, Jr. when Male stepped down last fall.)

http://www.mohonasen.org/mohonweb/new/new.html   5/31/99

Resource A

Many organizations can help educators with their public relations efforts. Contact any of the following:

American Association of School Administrators
1801 N. Moore Street
Arlington, VA 22209
(703) 528-0700
http://www.aasa.org

Capital Region BOCES Communications Service
6 British American Boulevard
Latham, NY 12110
(518) 786-3263

Educational Press Association of America
Rowan University
201 Mullica Hill Road
Glassboro, NJ 08028-1701
http://www.edpress.org

Education Week
6935 Arlington Road
Suite 100
Bethesda, MD 20814-5233
http://www.edweek.org

Institute for Participatory Management and Planning
Hans and Annemarie Bleiker
P.O. Box 1937
Monterey, CA 93942-1937
(831) 373-4292
http://www.ipmp-bleiker.com

National Parent Teachers Association
330 N. Wabash Avenue
Suite 2100
Chicago, IL 60611
(312) 670-6782
http://www.pta.org

National School Public Relations Association
15948 Derwood Road
Rockville, MD 20855
(301) 519-0496
http://www.nspra.org

Public Relations Society of America
33 Irving Place
New York, NY 10003-2376
(212) 995-2230
http://www.prsa.org

References

Airport Authority of Washoe County. (1999, Winter). *Airport Flyer.*

Albany Medical Center. (1995, May/June). Albany high students get glimpse into life at AMC. *Center News.*

Bleiker, H., & Bleiker, A. (1997). *Citizen participation handbook for public officials and other professionals working in the public sector.* Monterey, CA: Institute for Participatory Management and Planning.

City School District of Albany. (1994, March/April). *Capital Education.*

Cox, J. (n.d.). *Developing credibility tips.* Albany, NY: Capital Region BOCES Communications Service.

Gunnison Watershed School District RE1J. (1996-1997). *Accountability report.* Gunnison, CO: Author.

Struggling with the anguish. (1998, May 23). *The Oregonian,* p. 1.

Washoe County School District. (1998, August). *Parents, 5*(1).

Williamalane, City of Springfield, & Springfield Public Schools. (n.d.). *Team Springfield.*